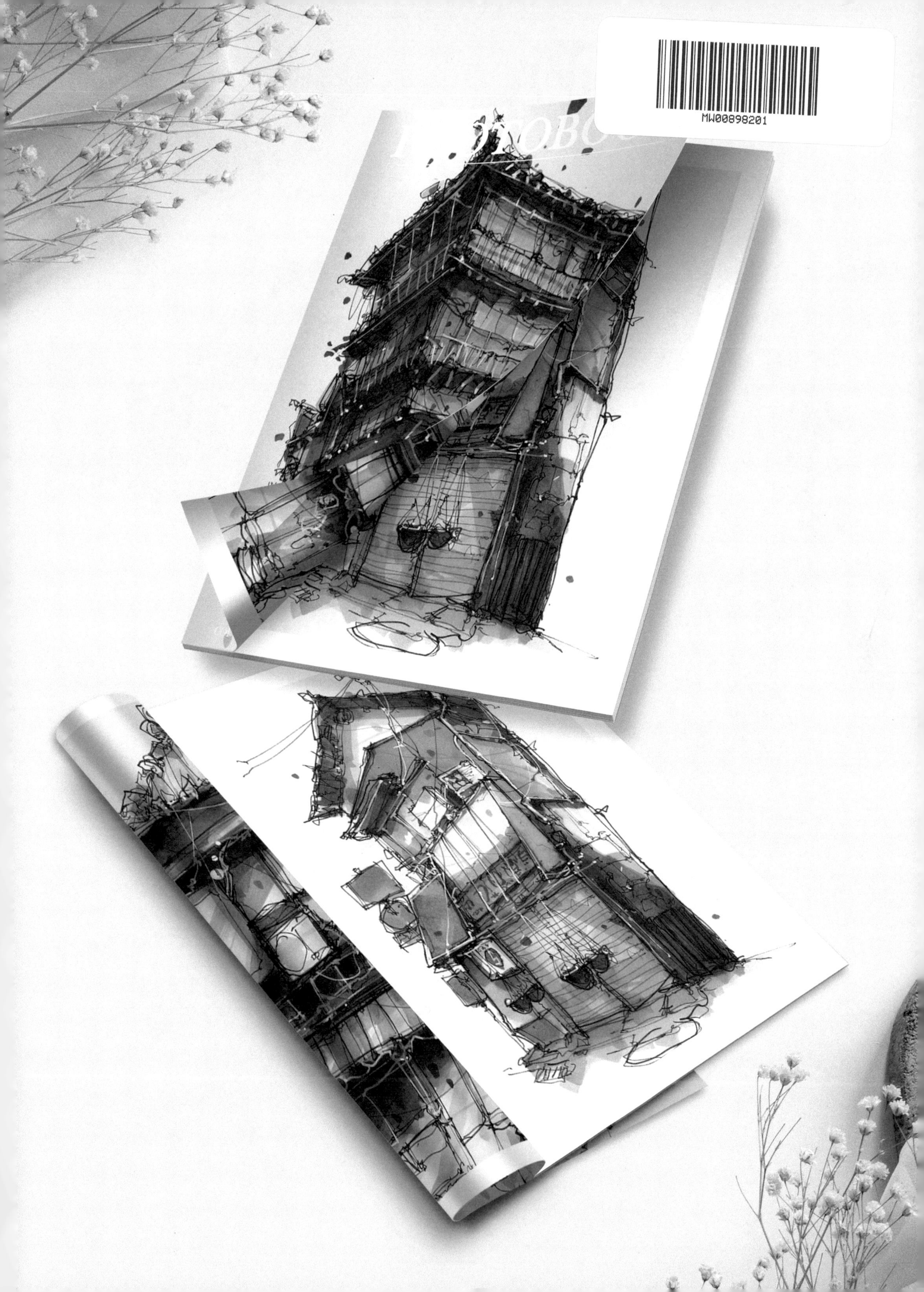

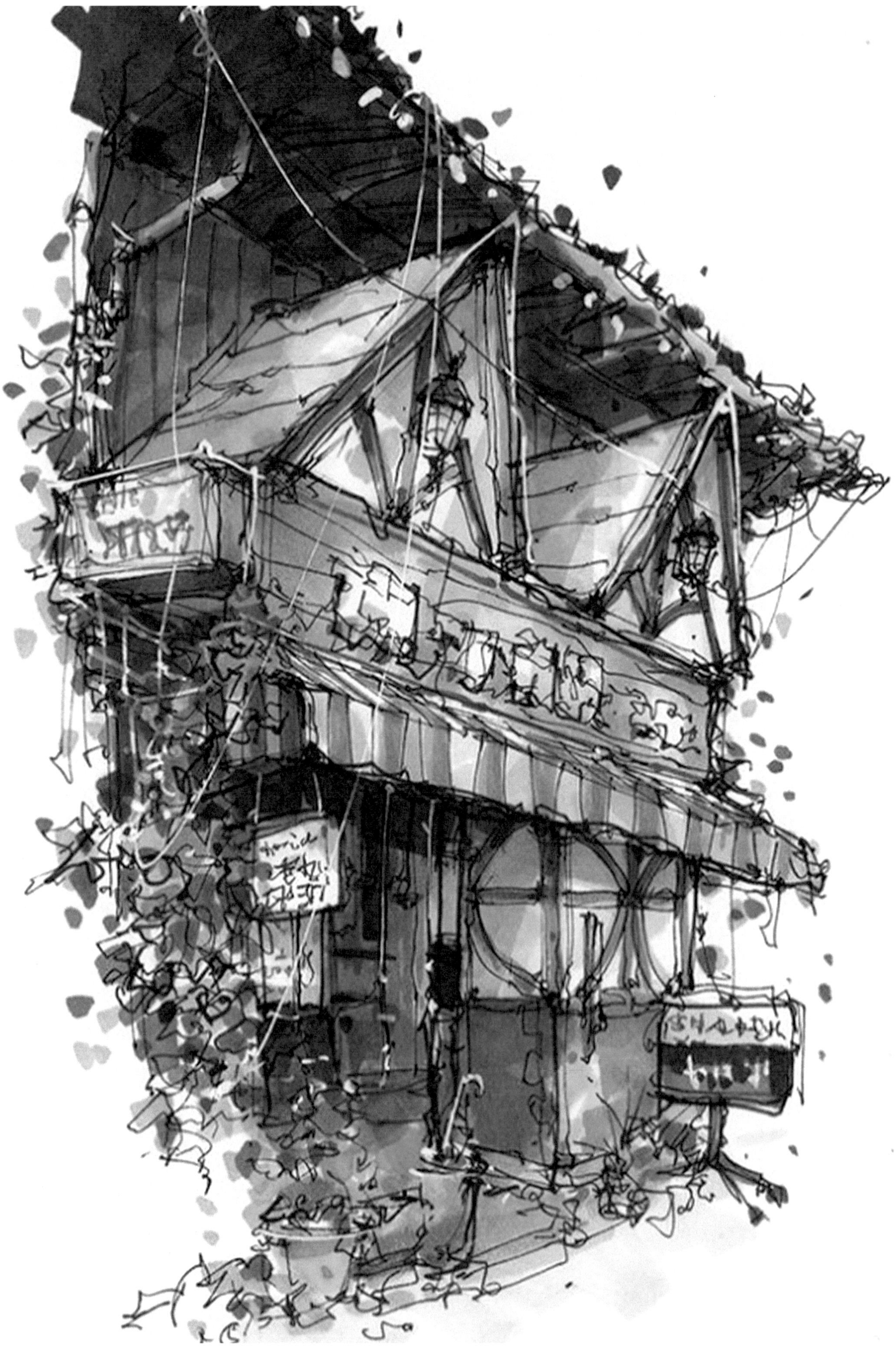

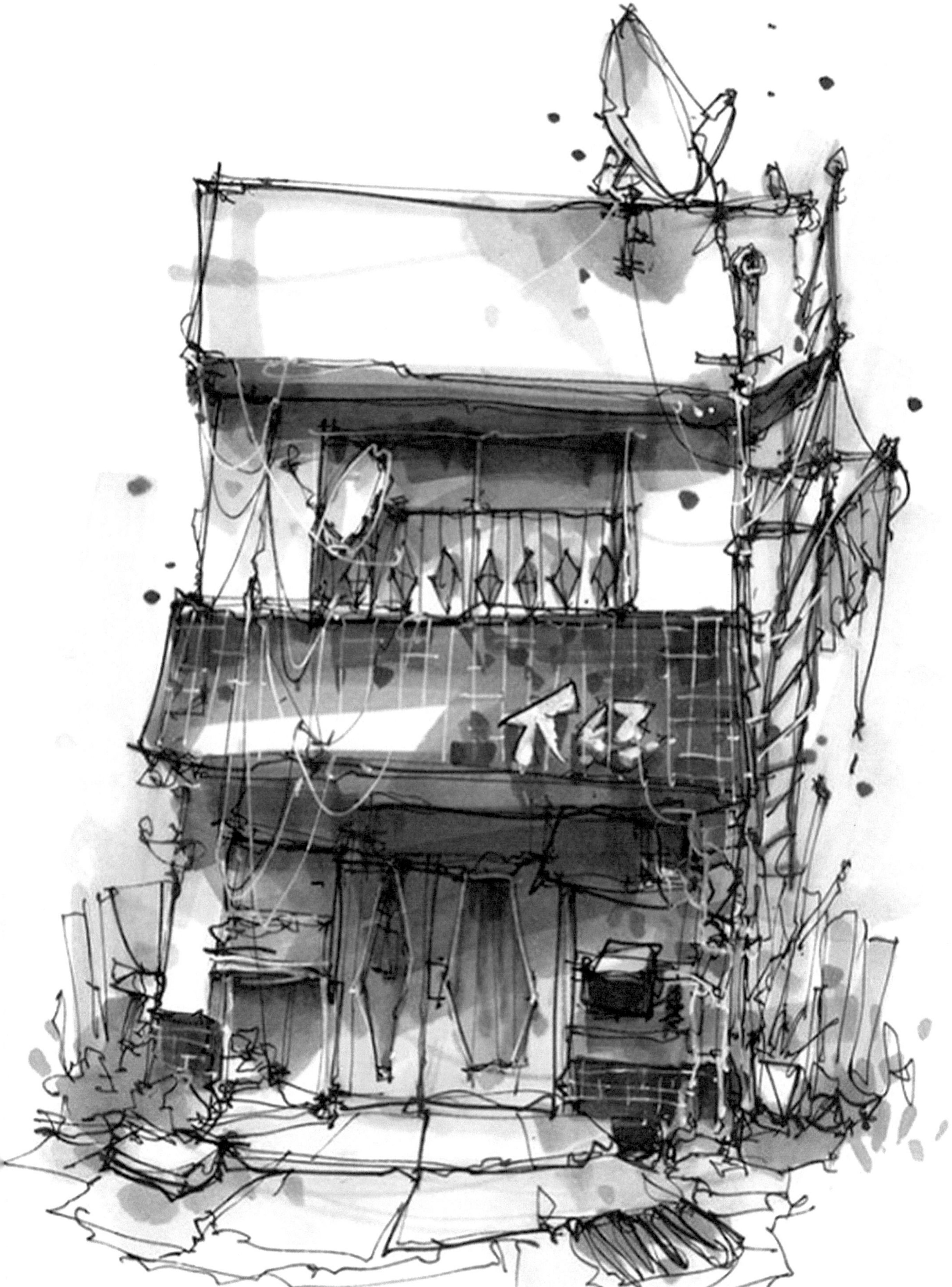

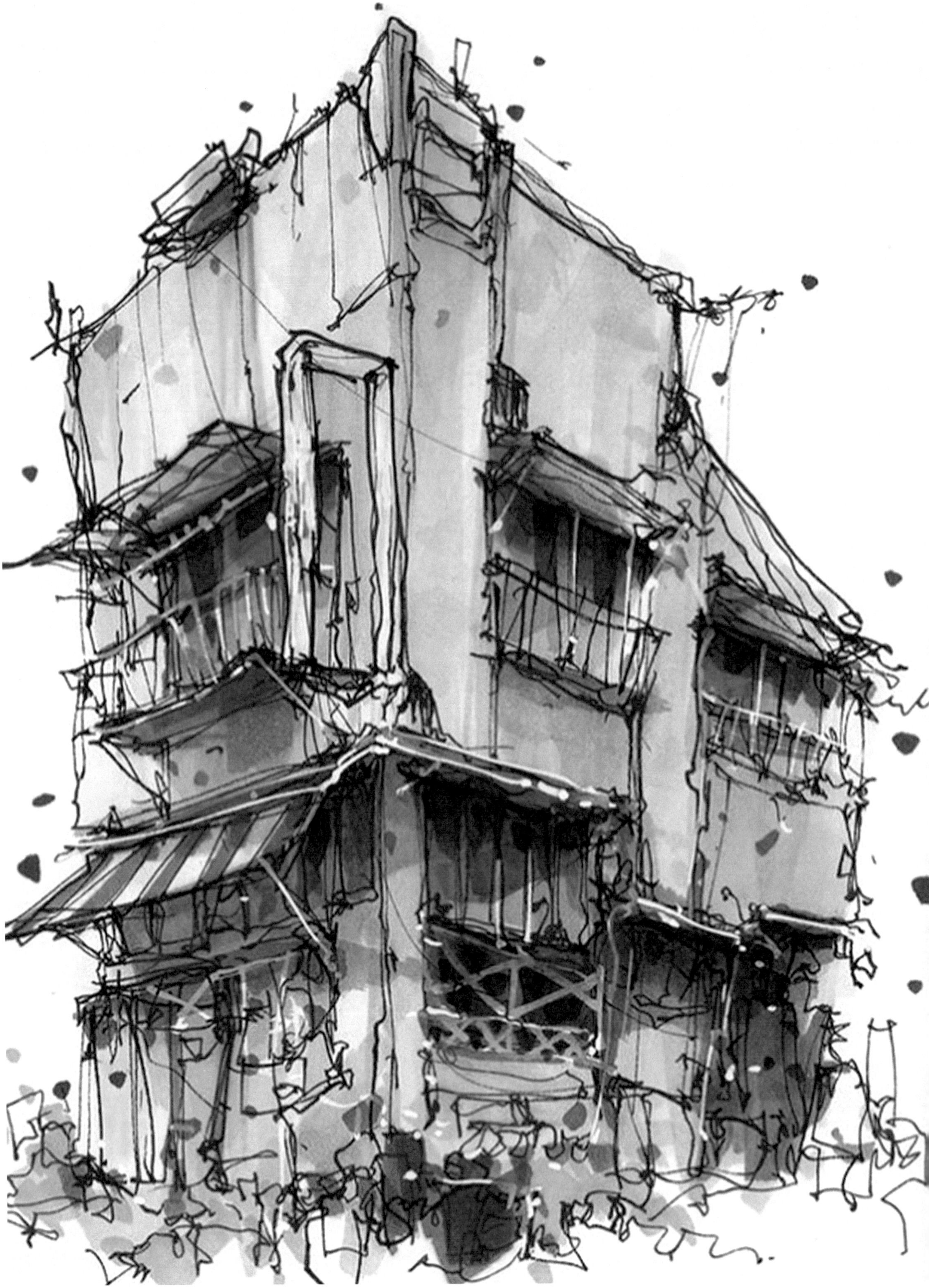

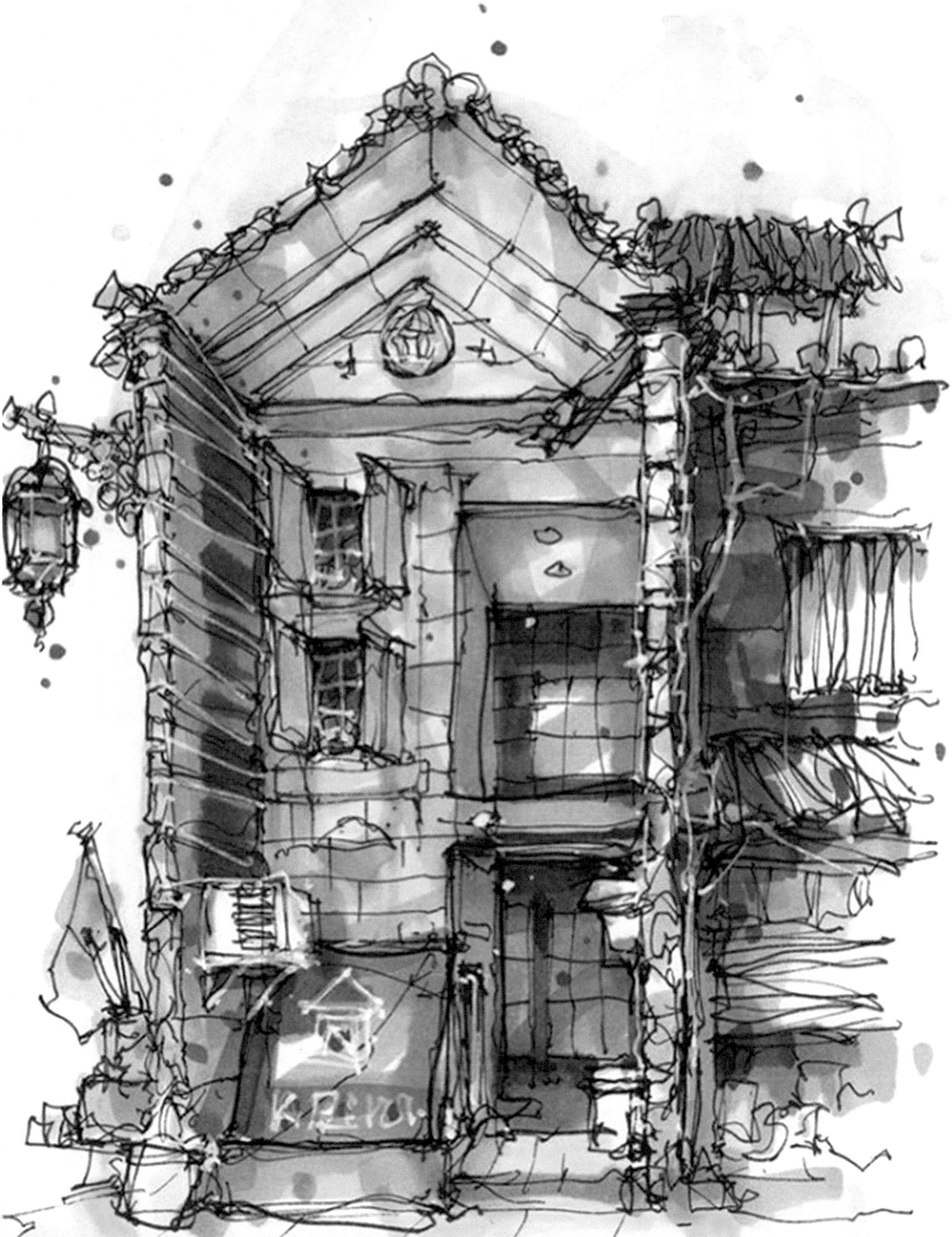

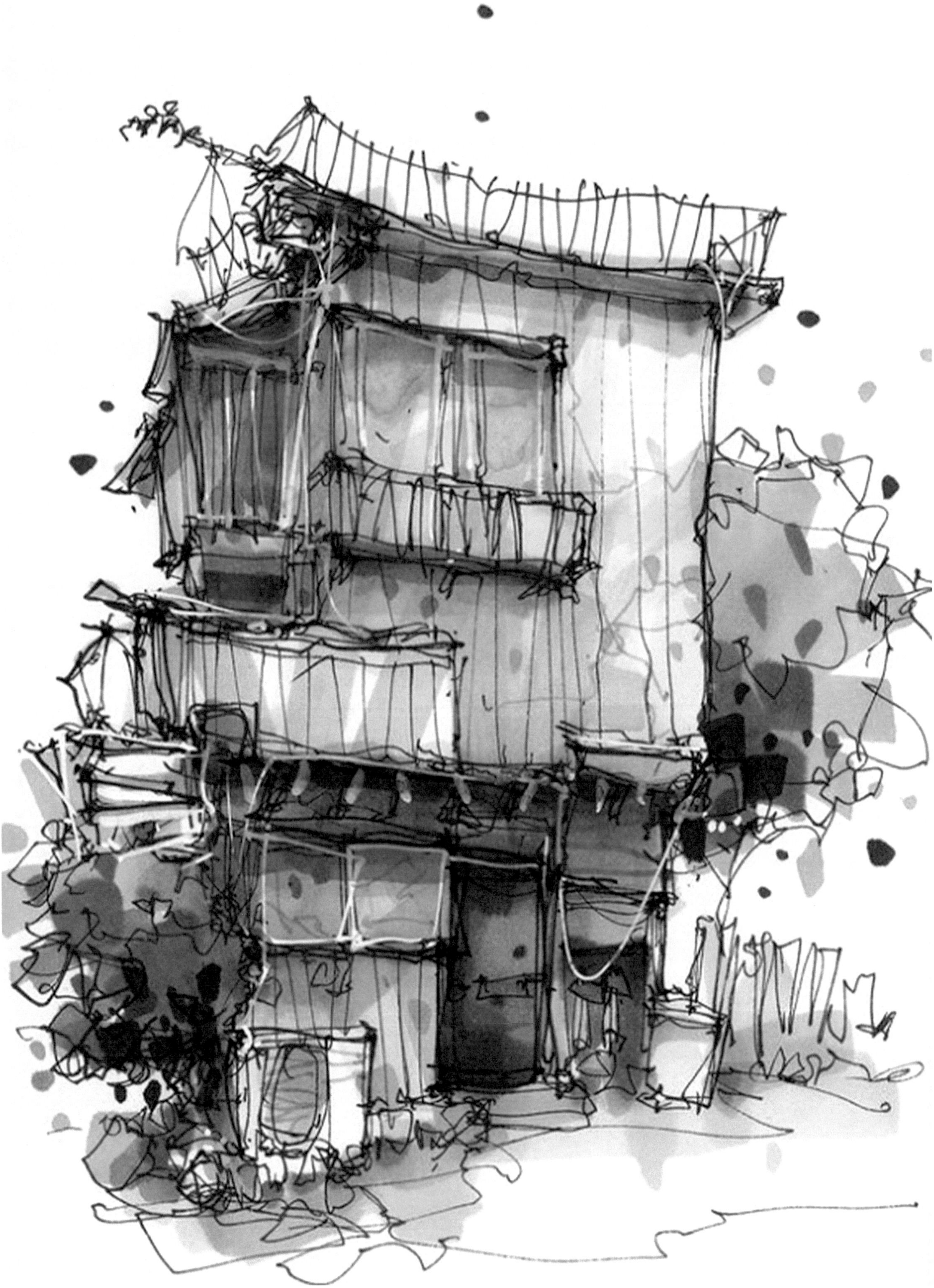

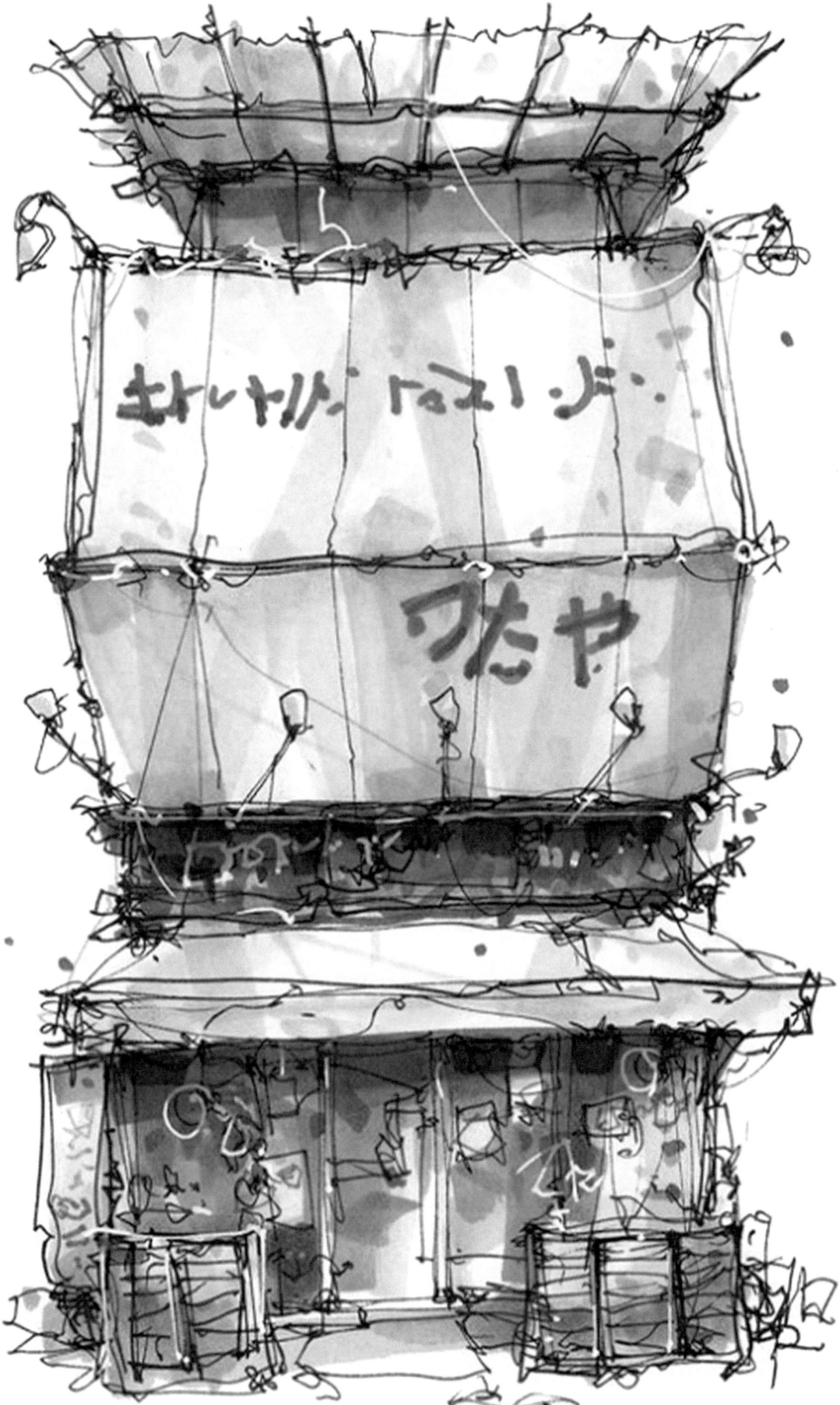
ワたや

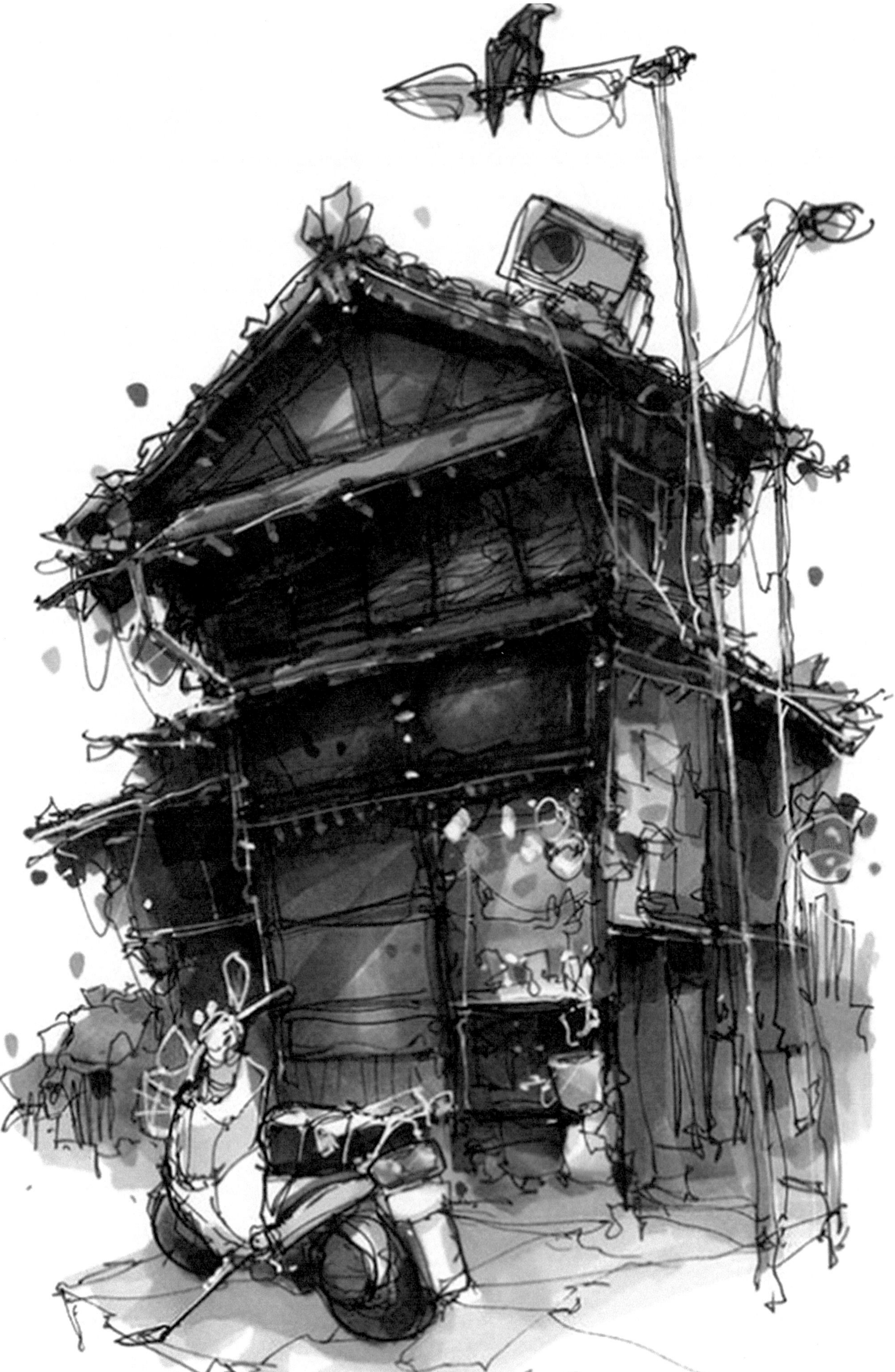

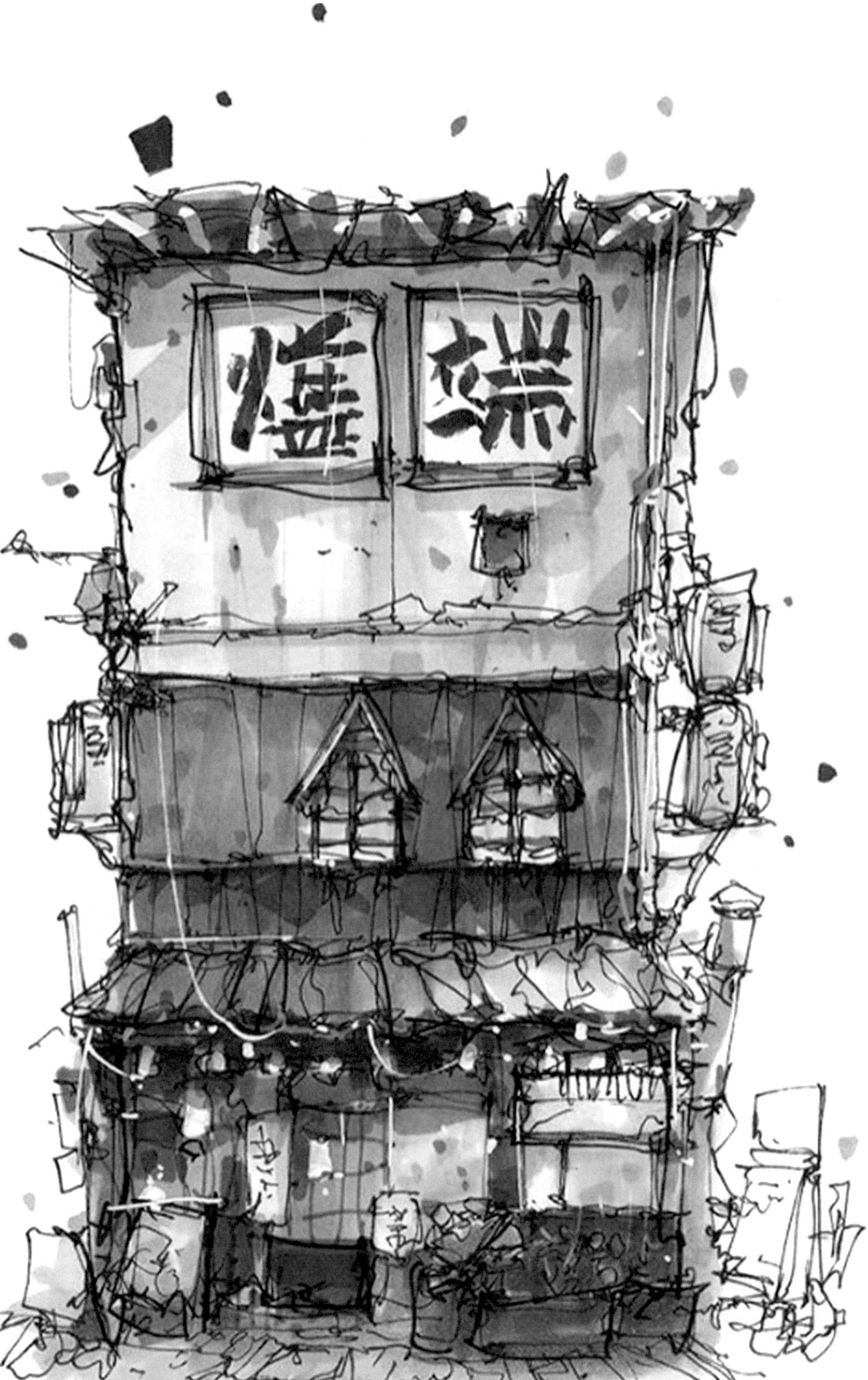

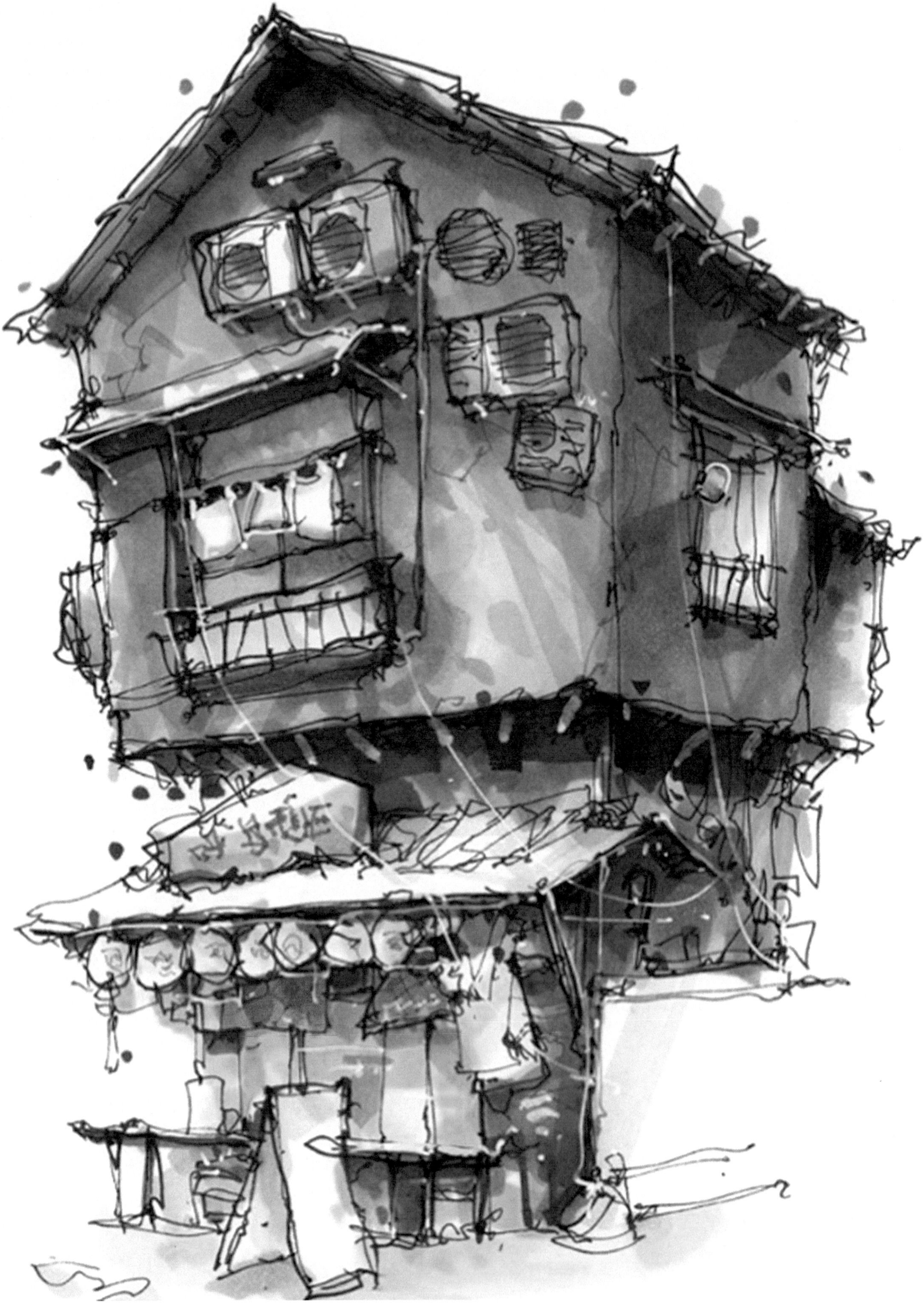

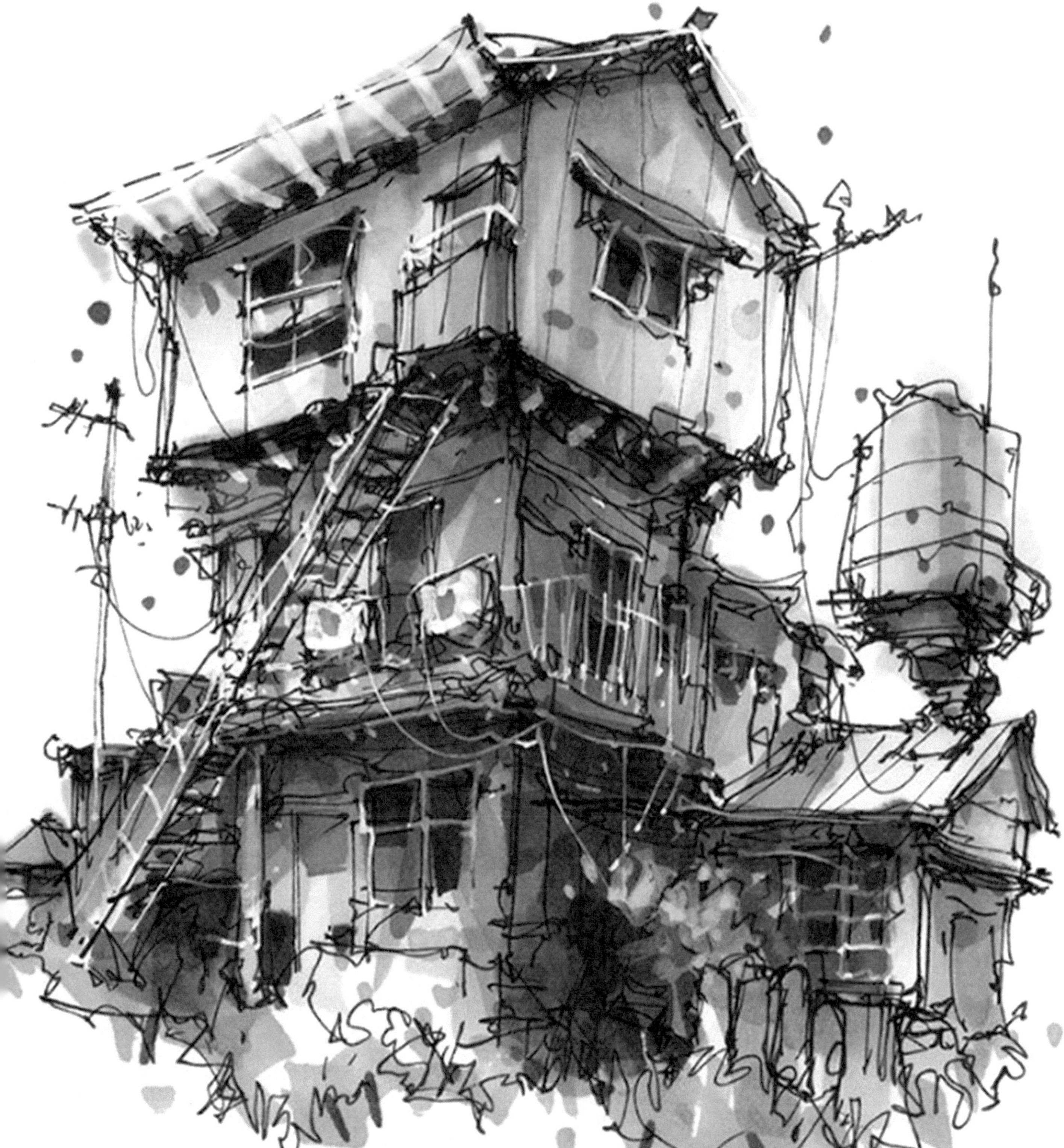

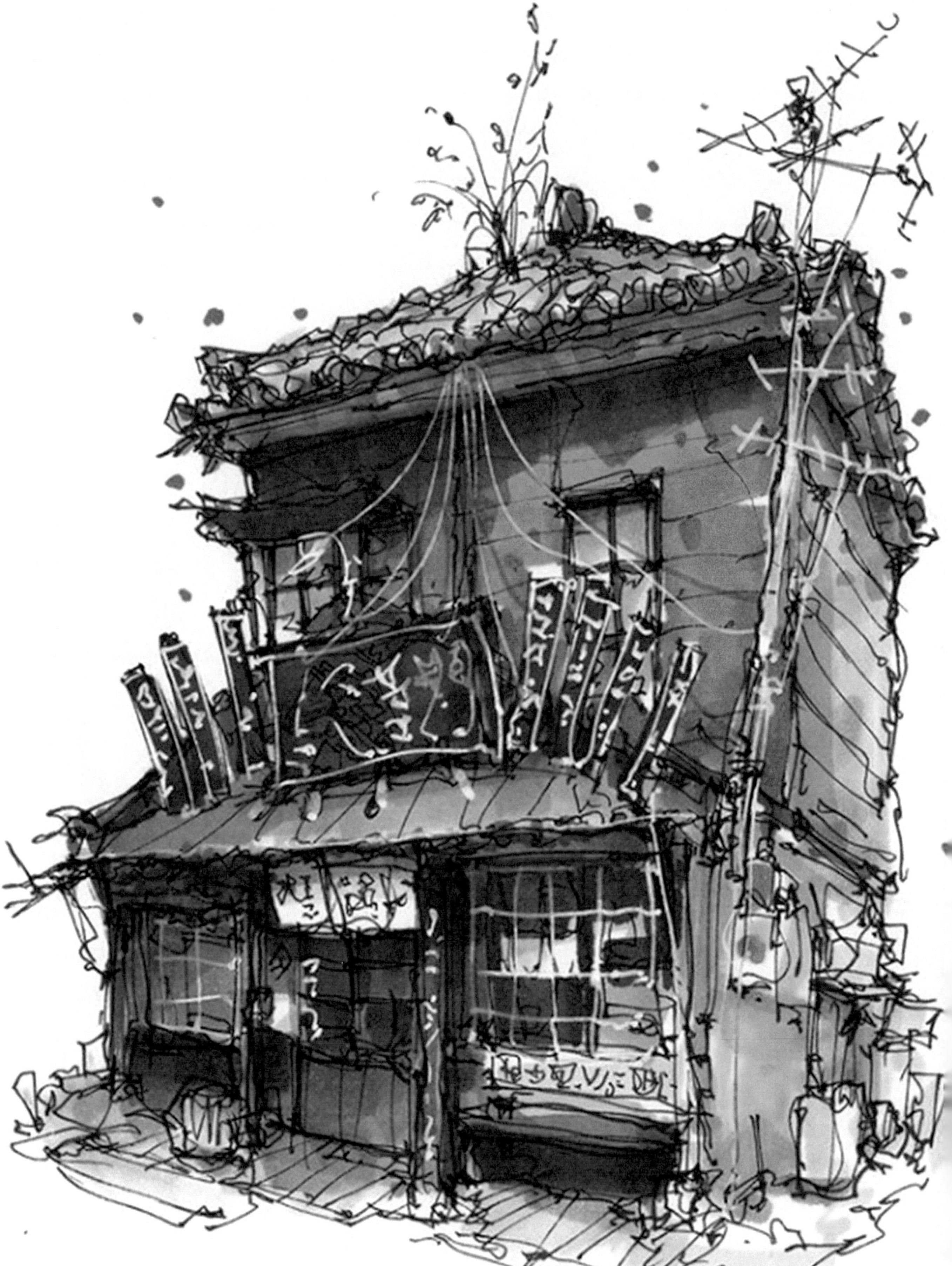

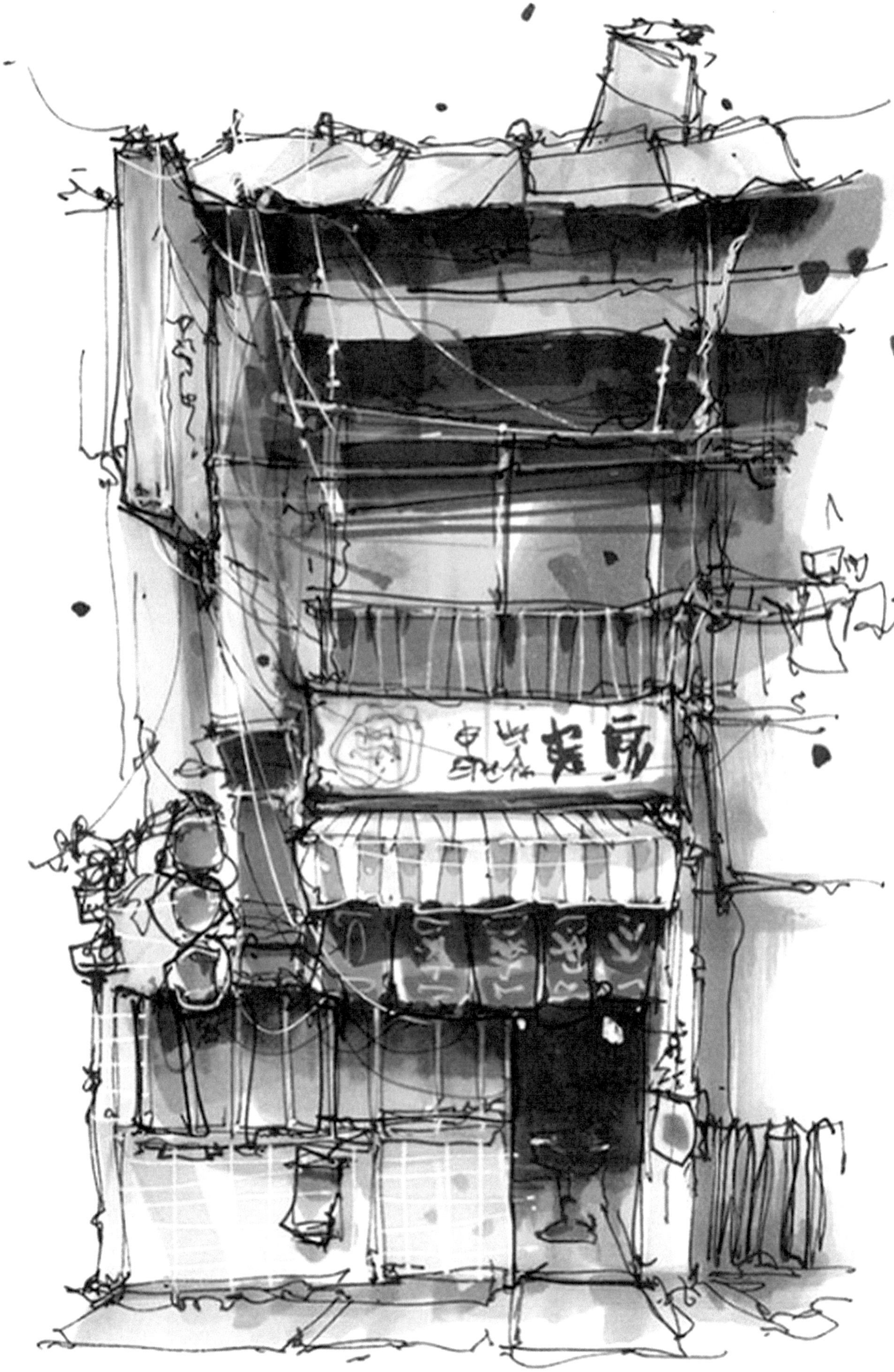

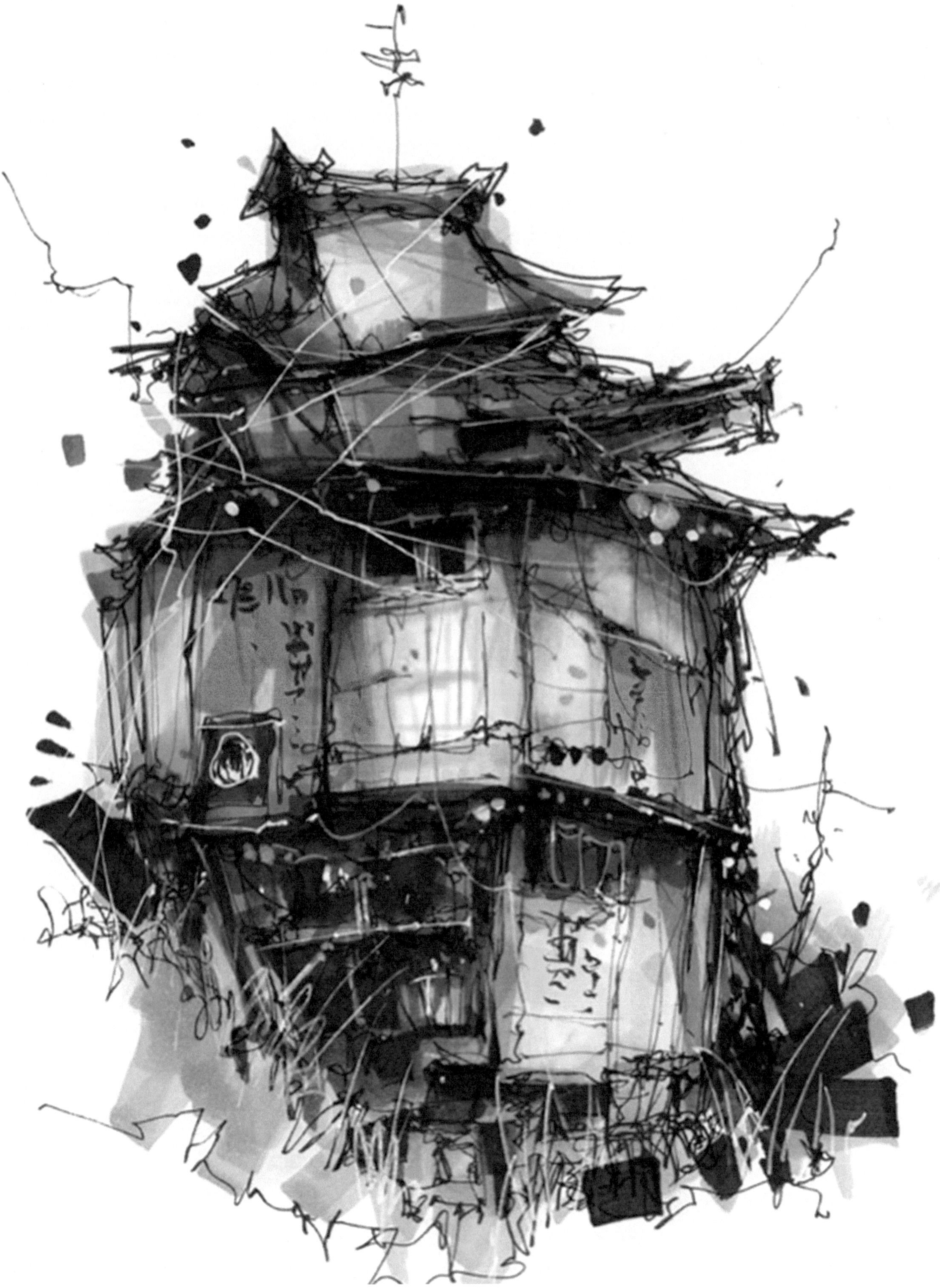

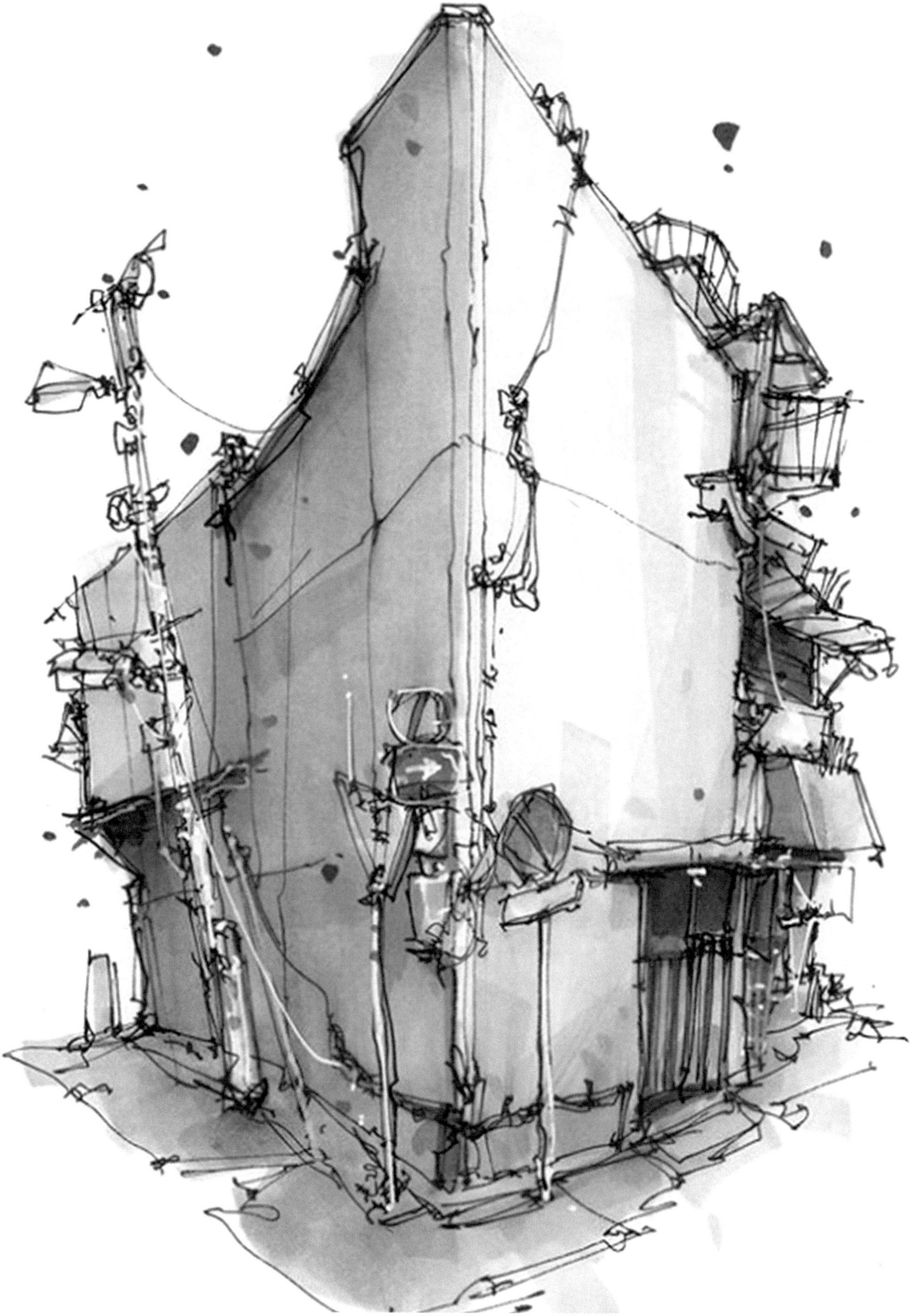

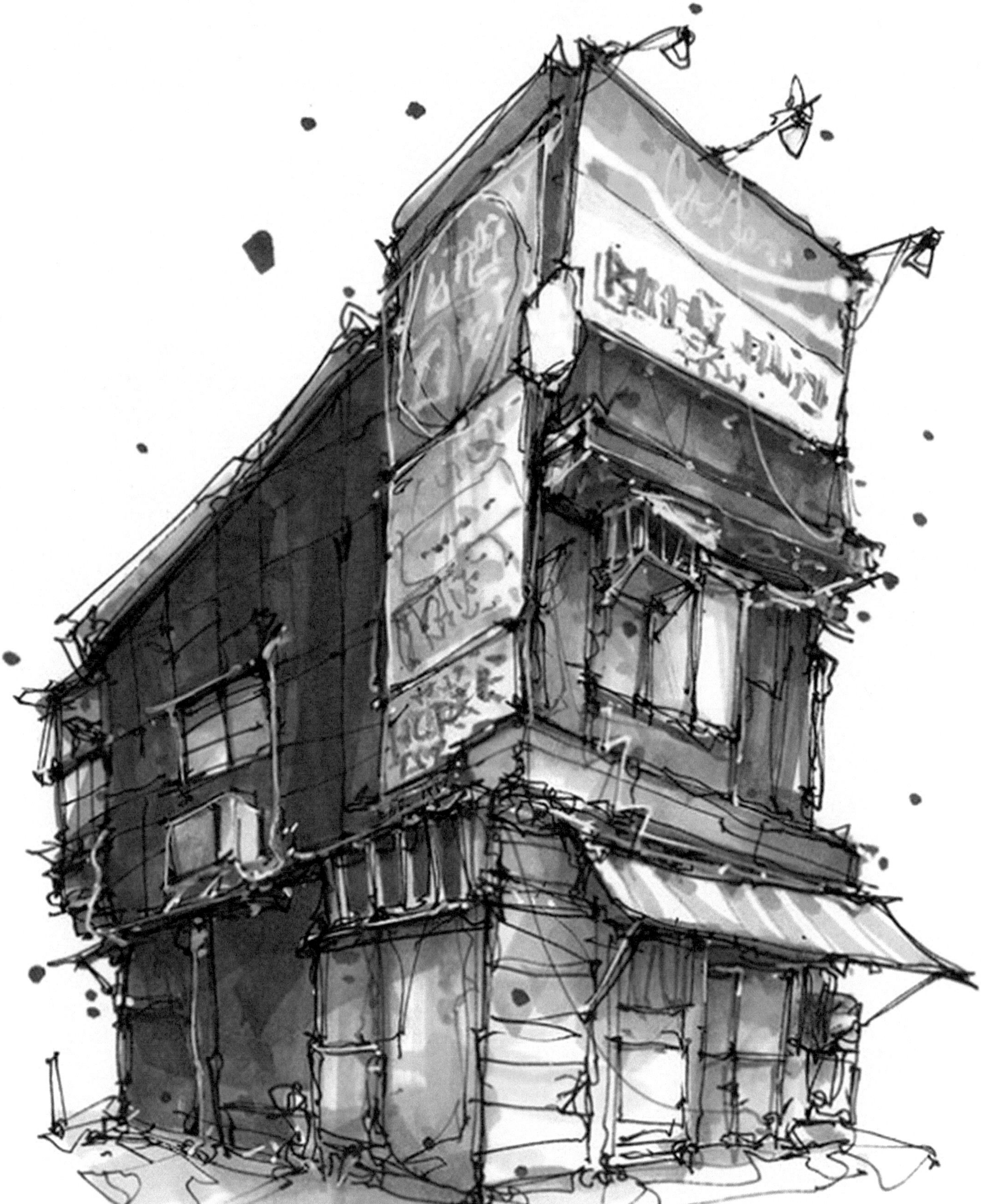

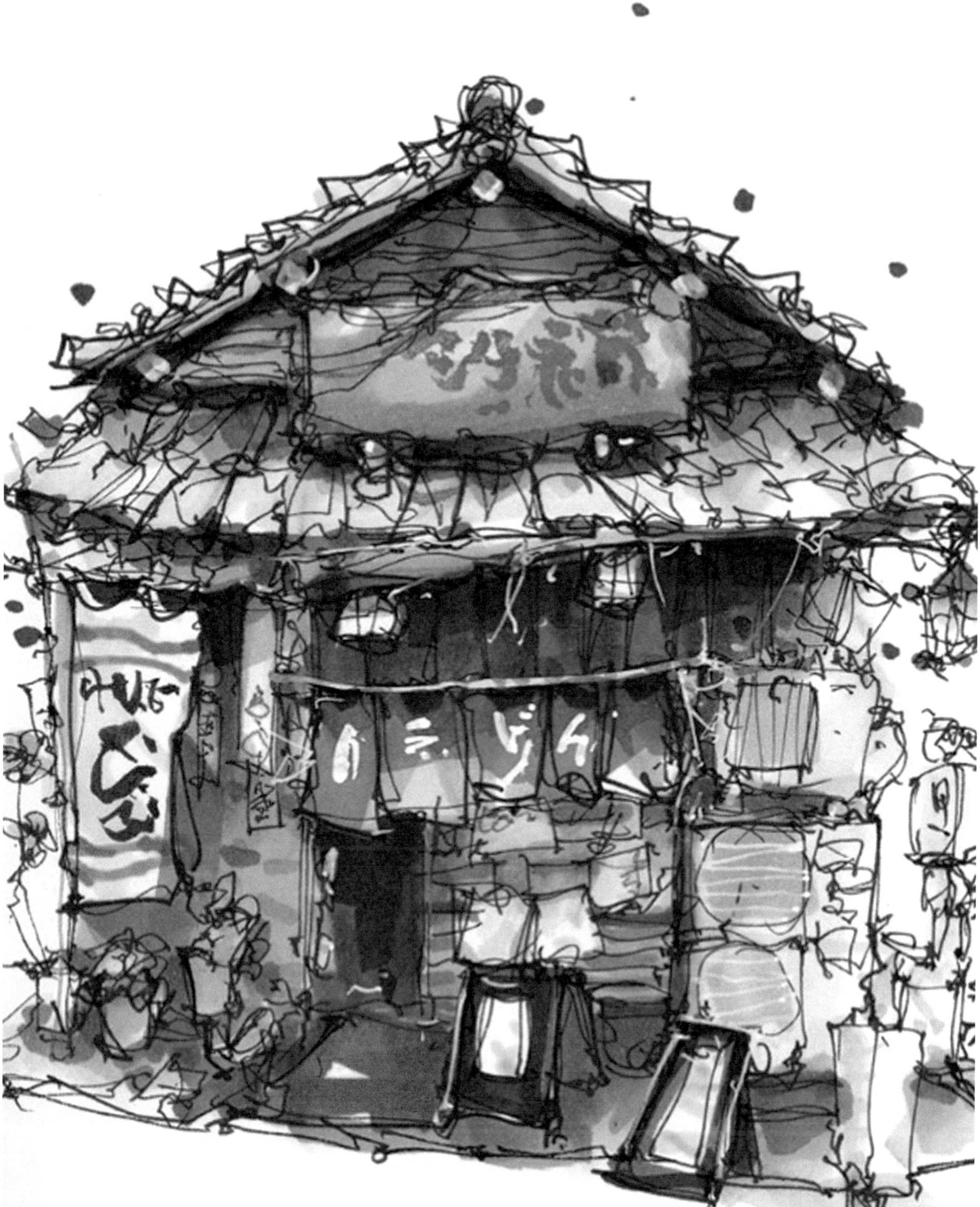

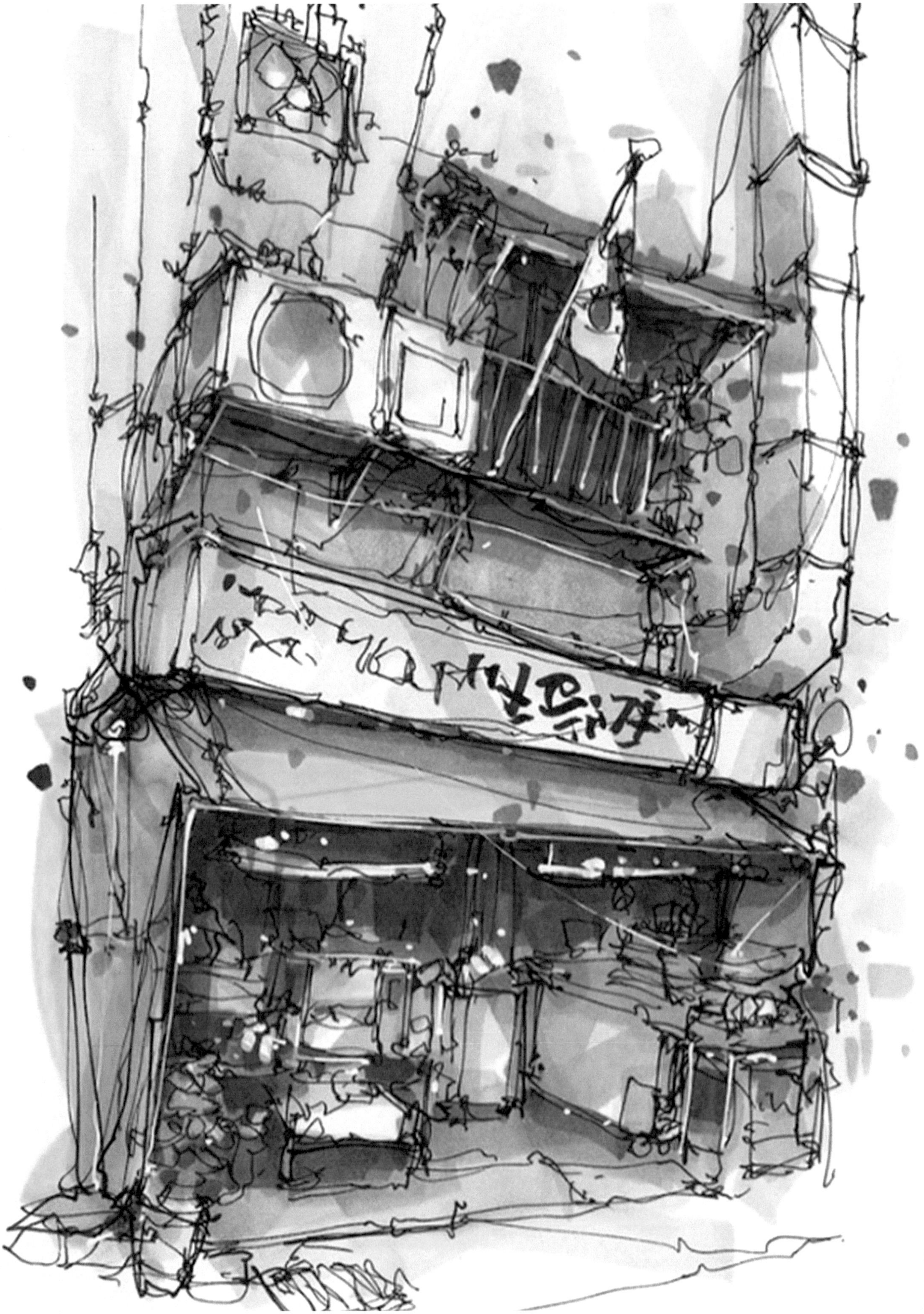

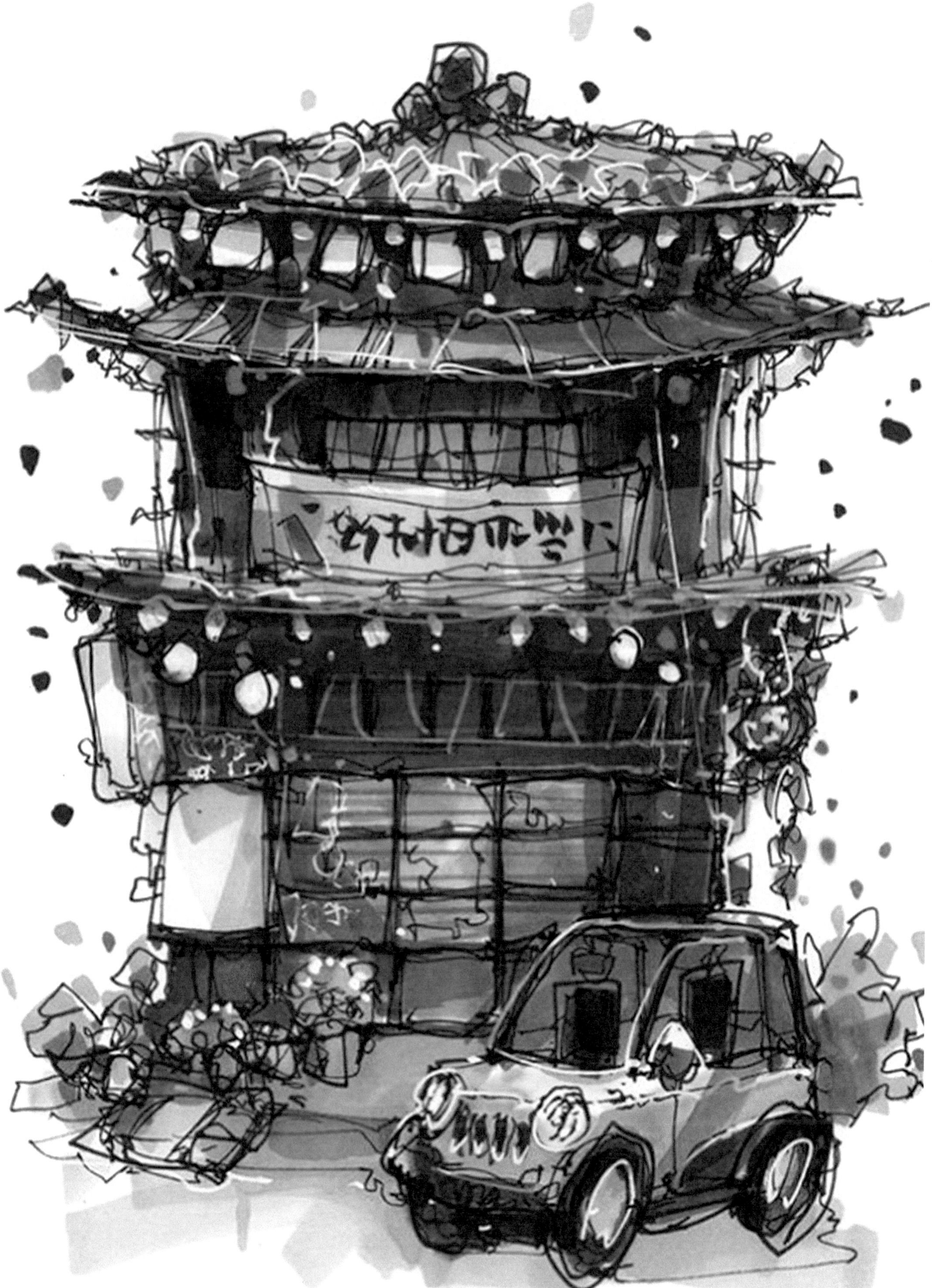

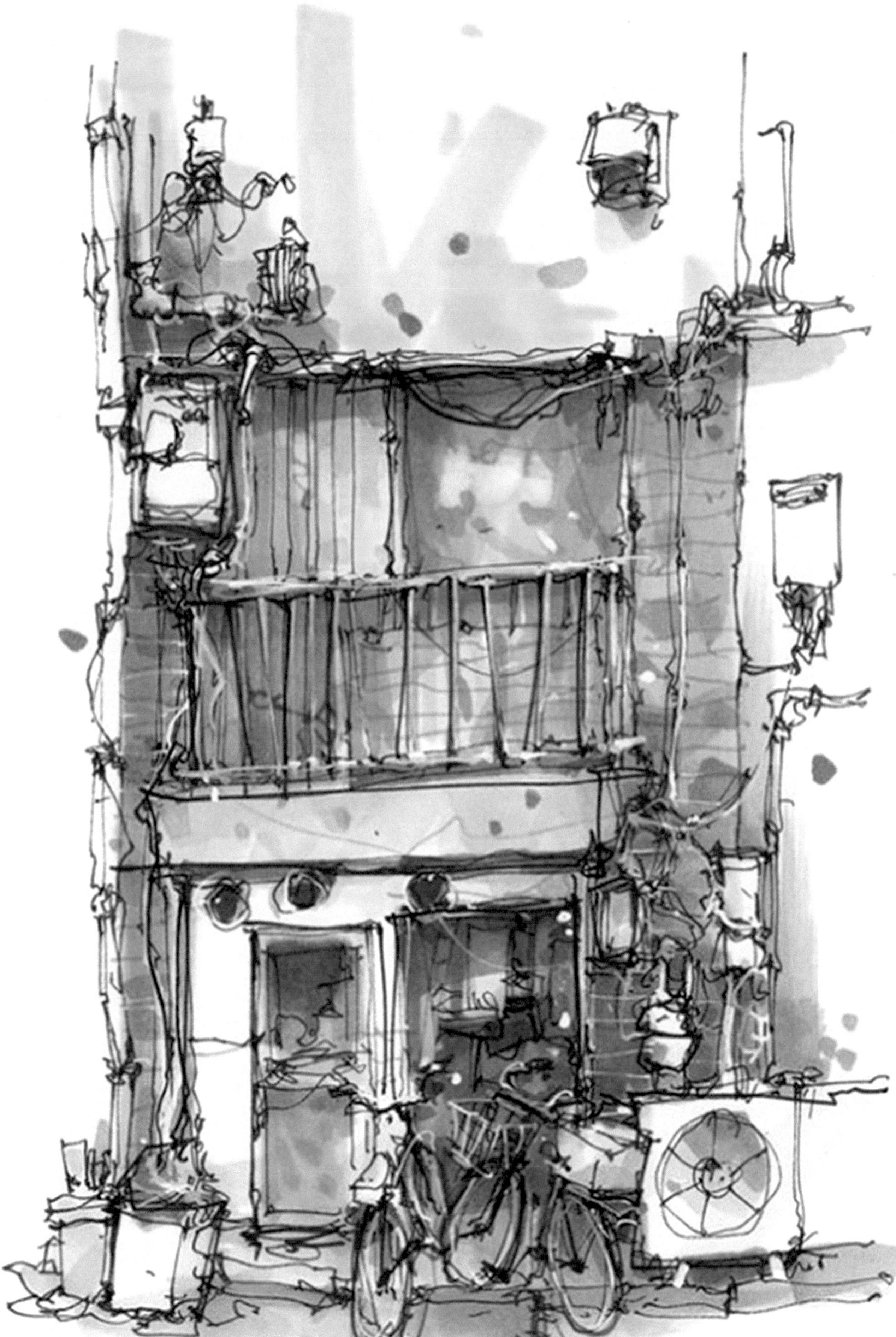

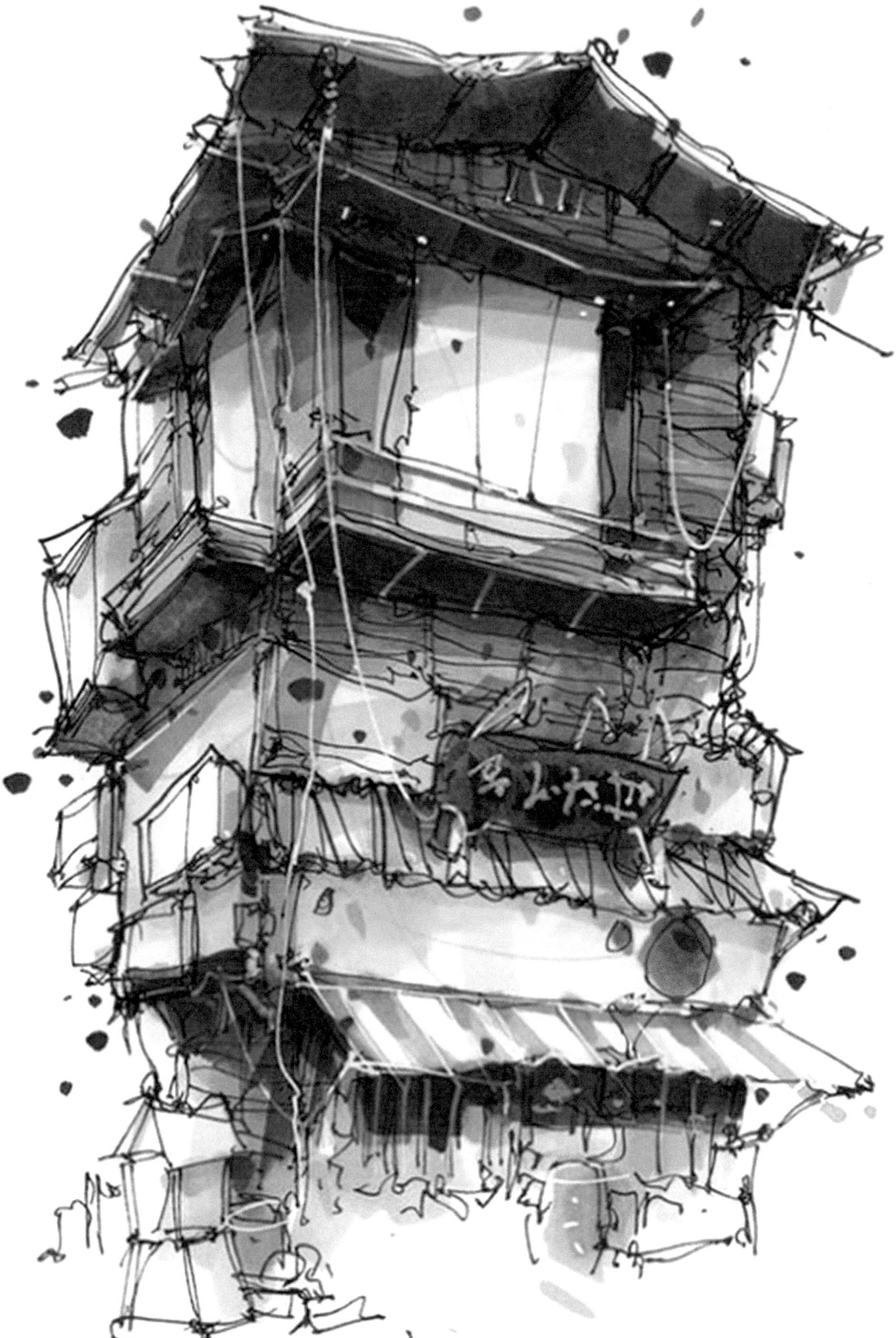

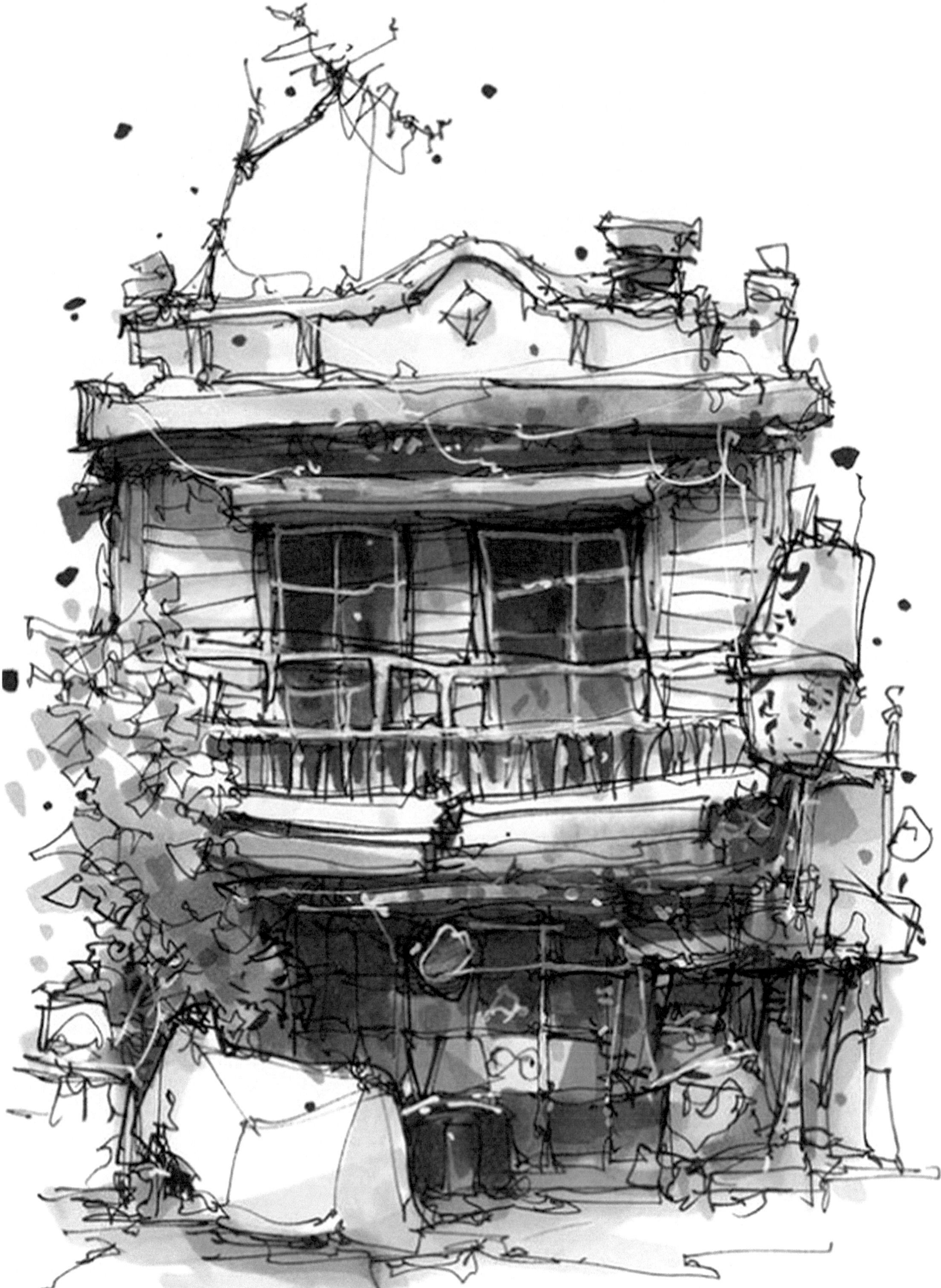

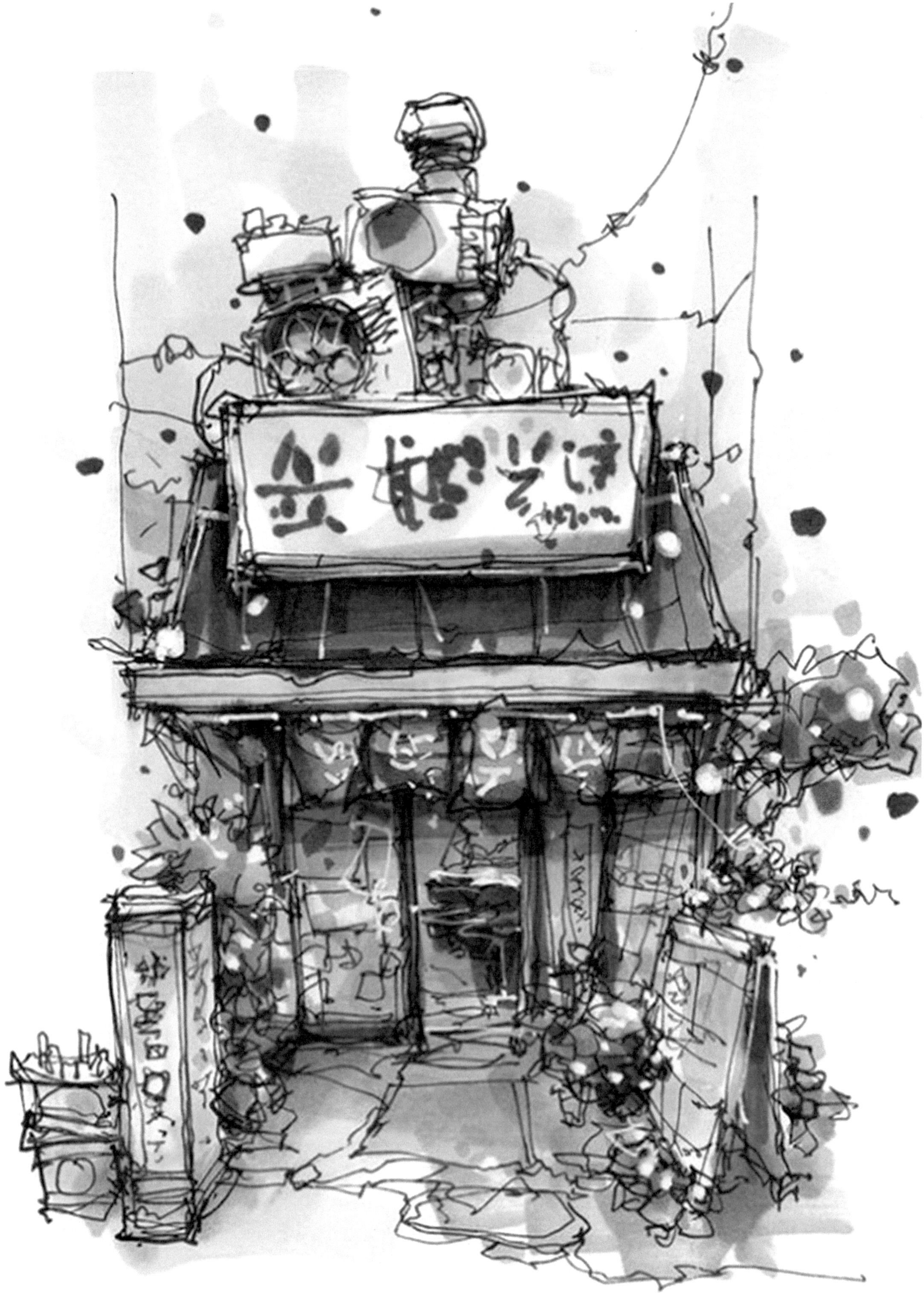

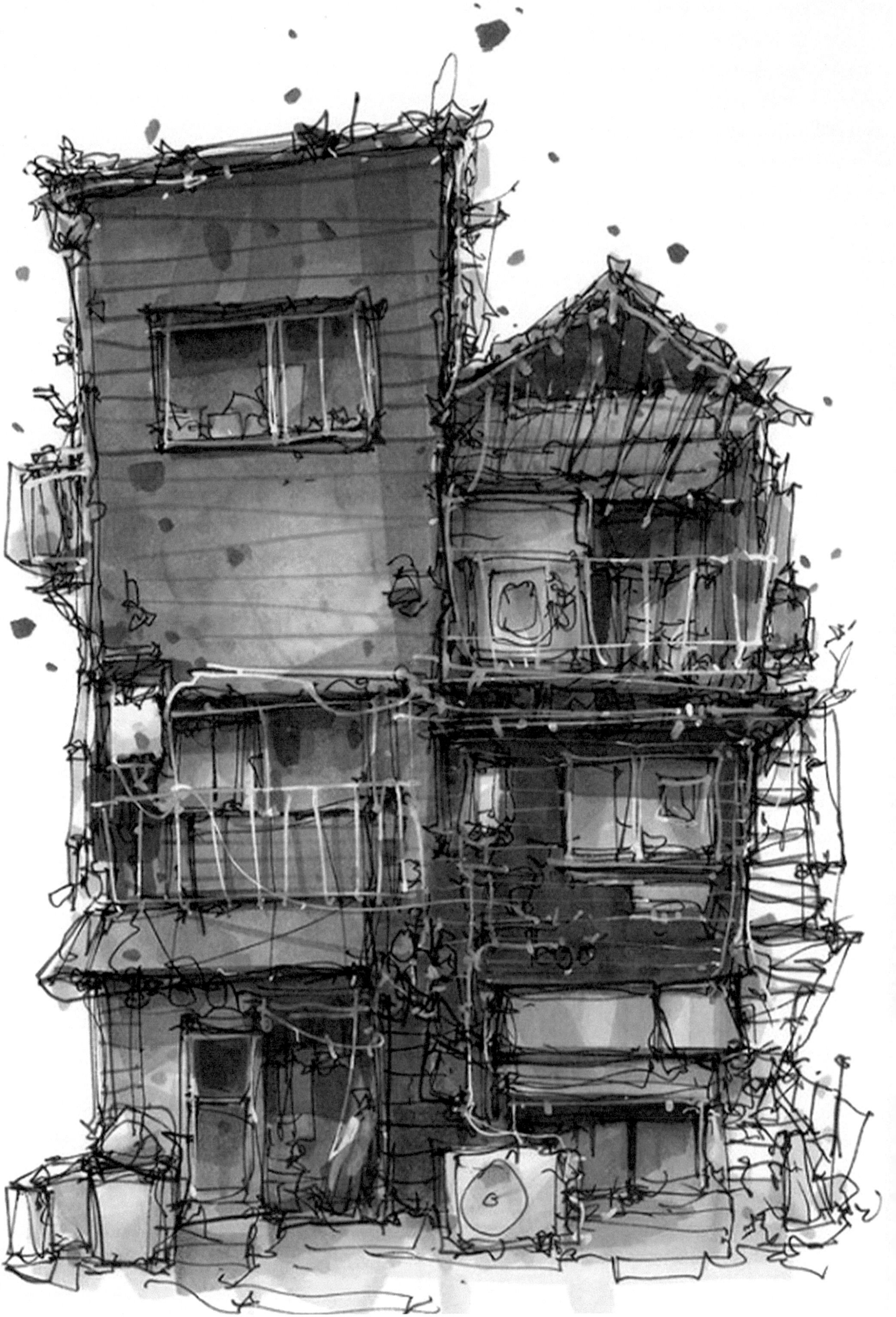

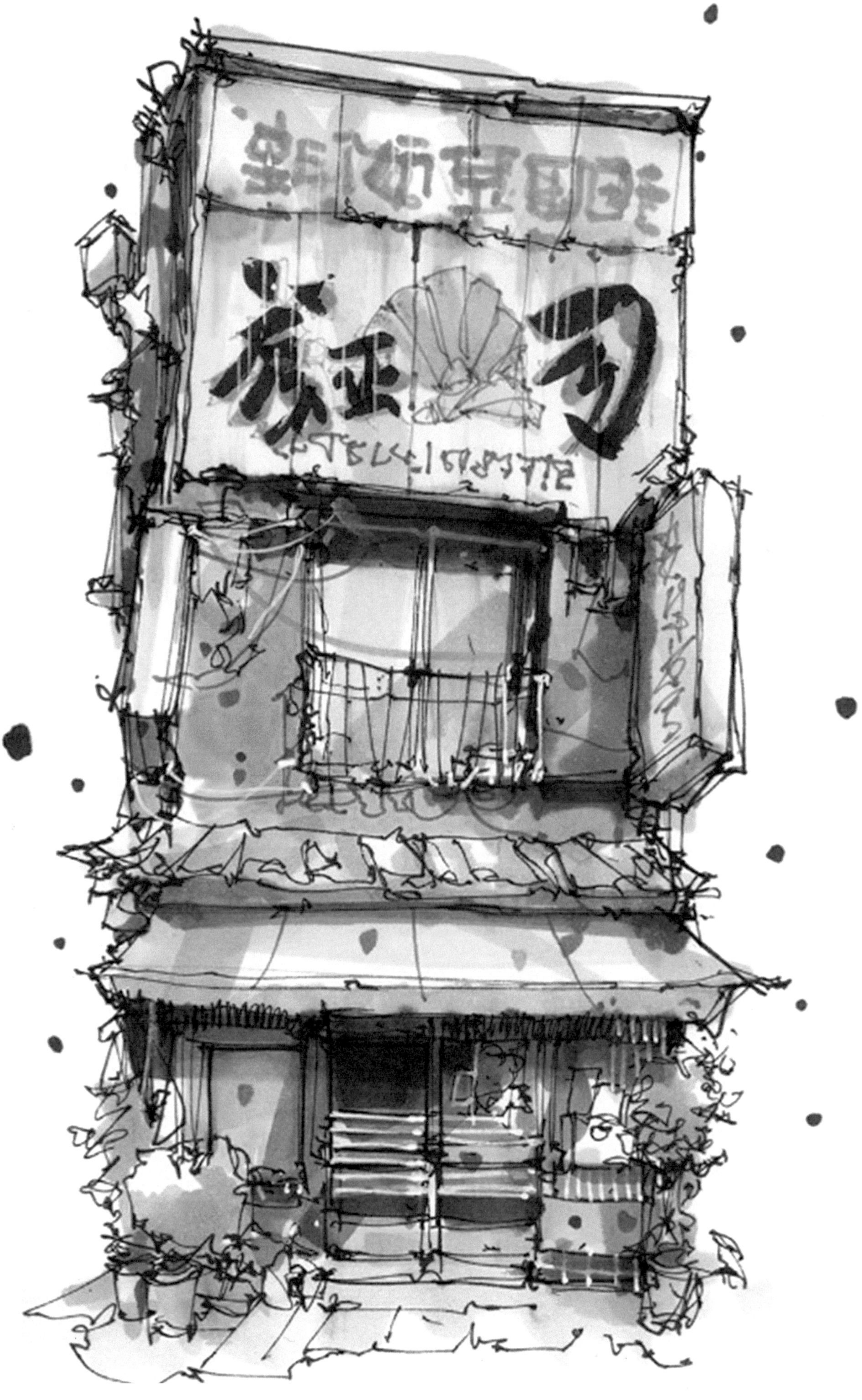

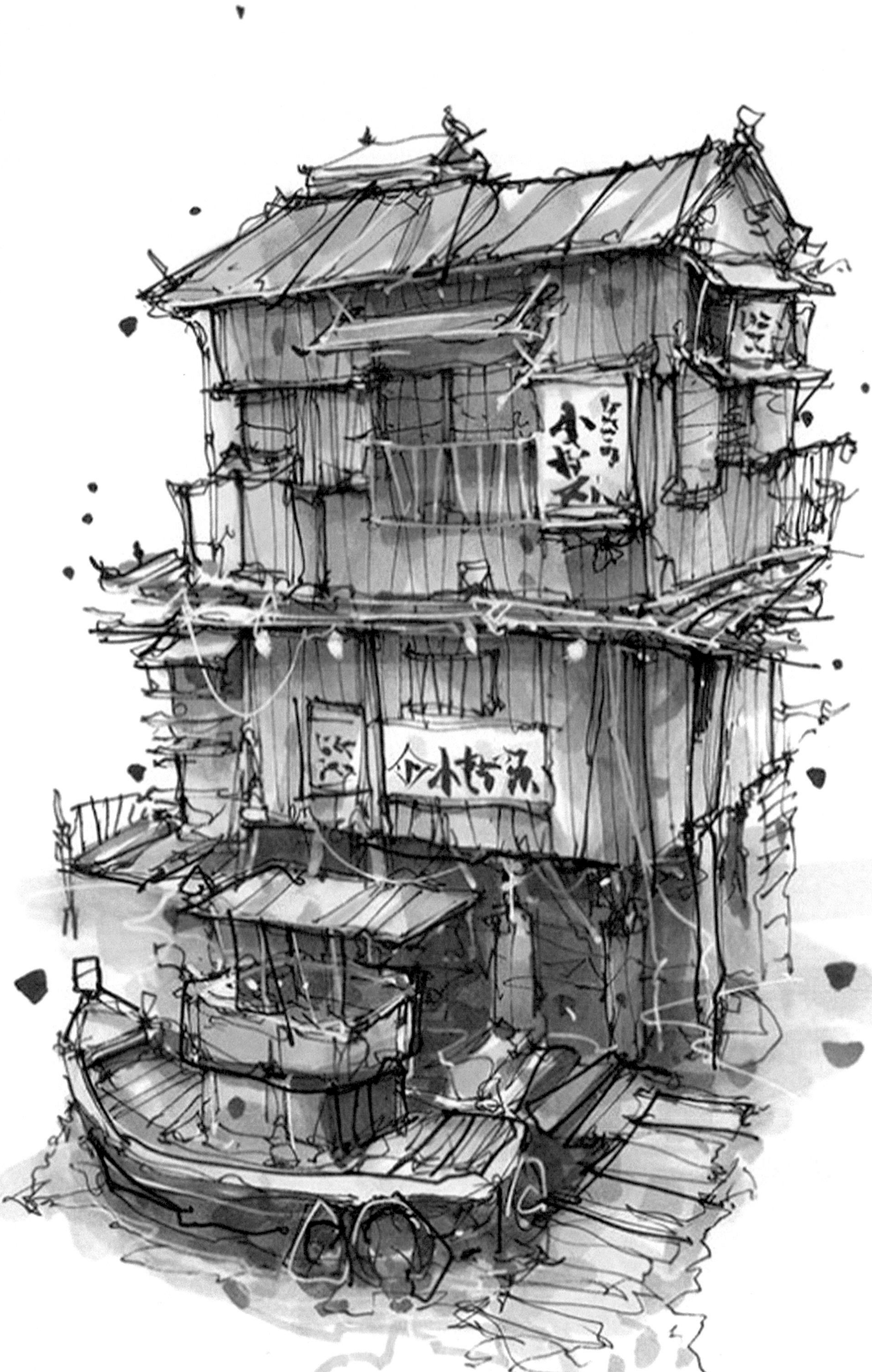

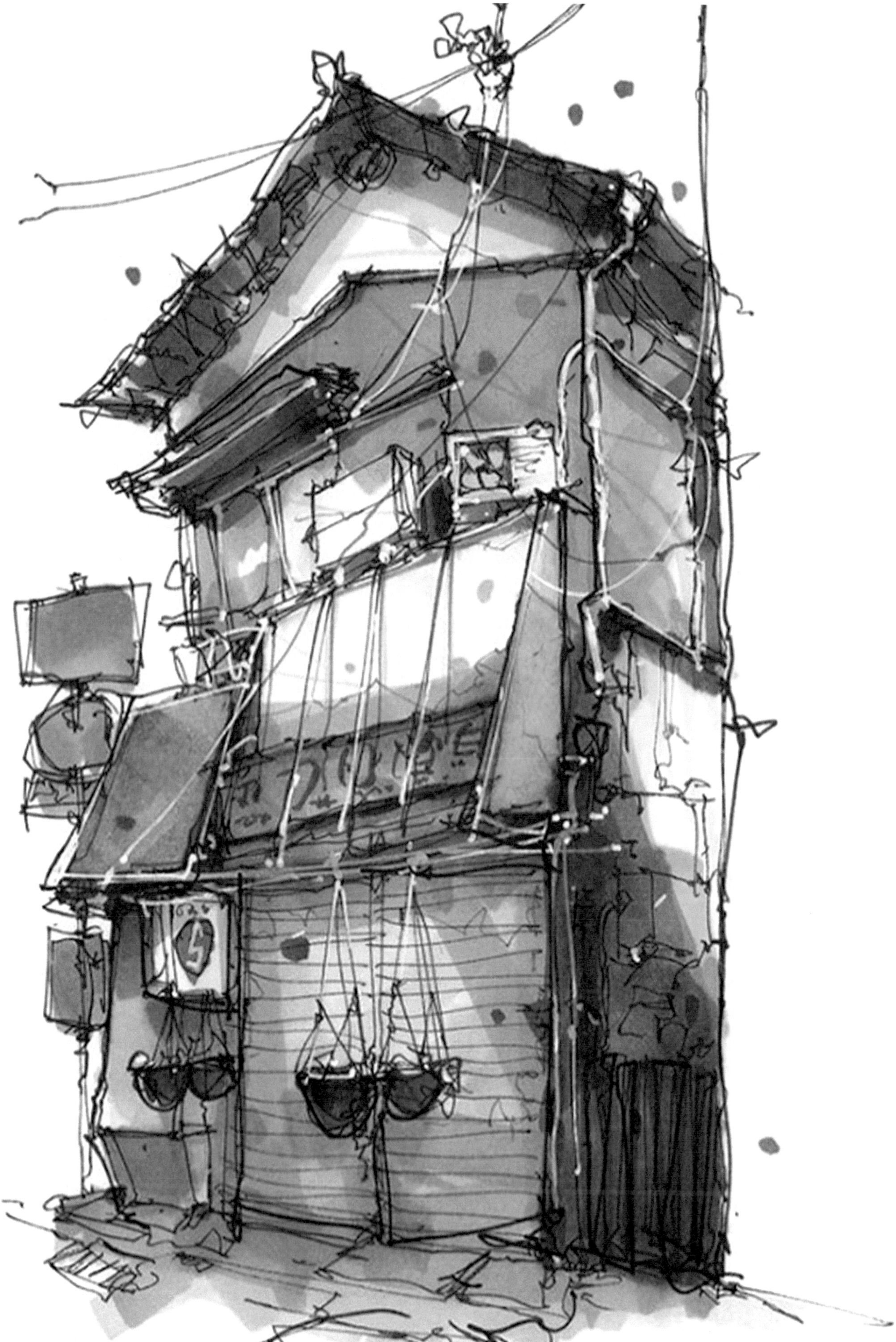

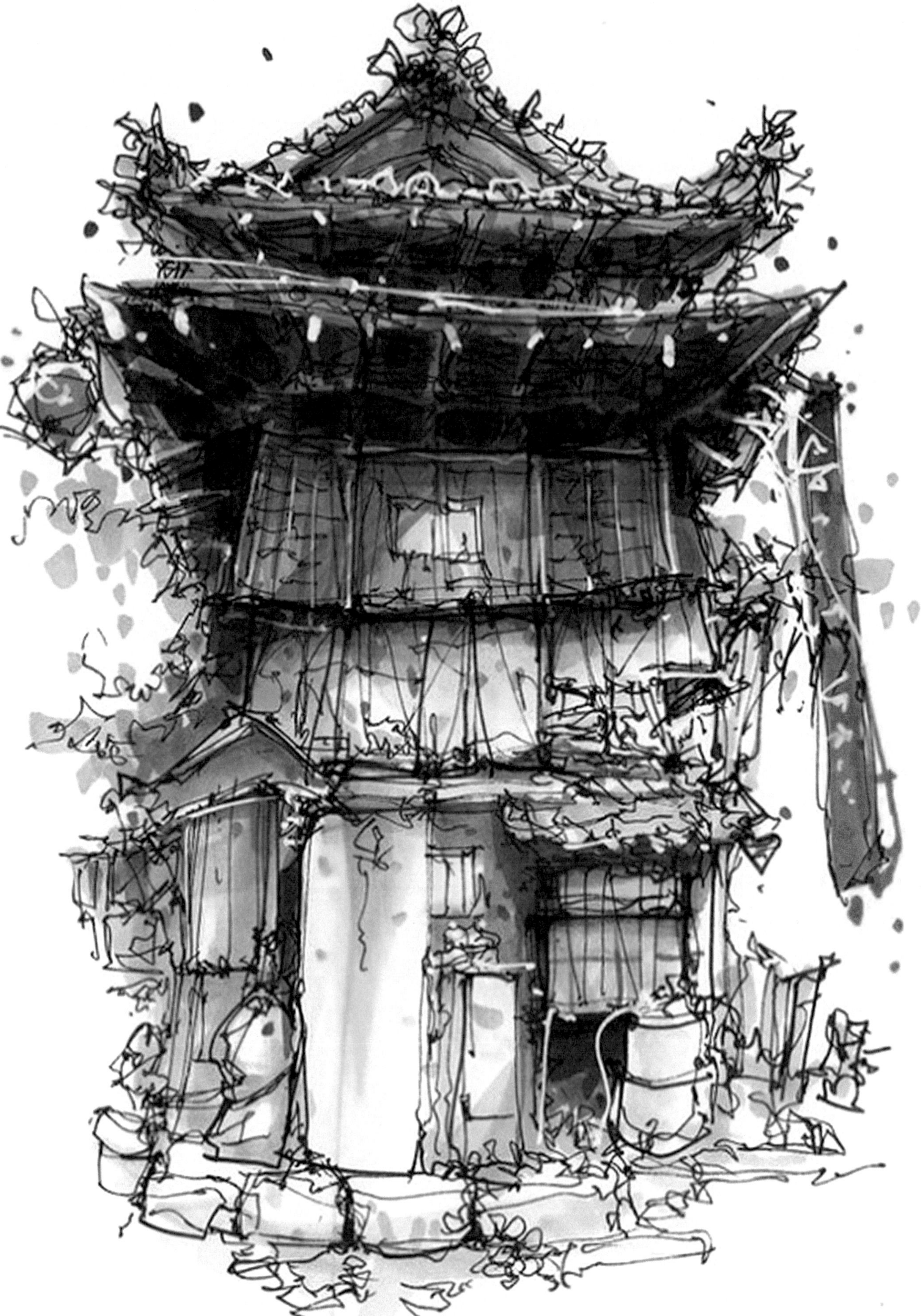

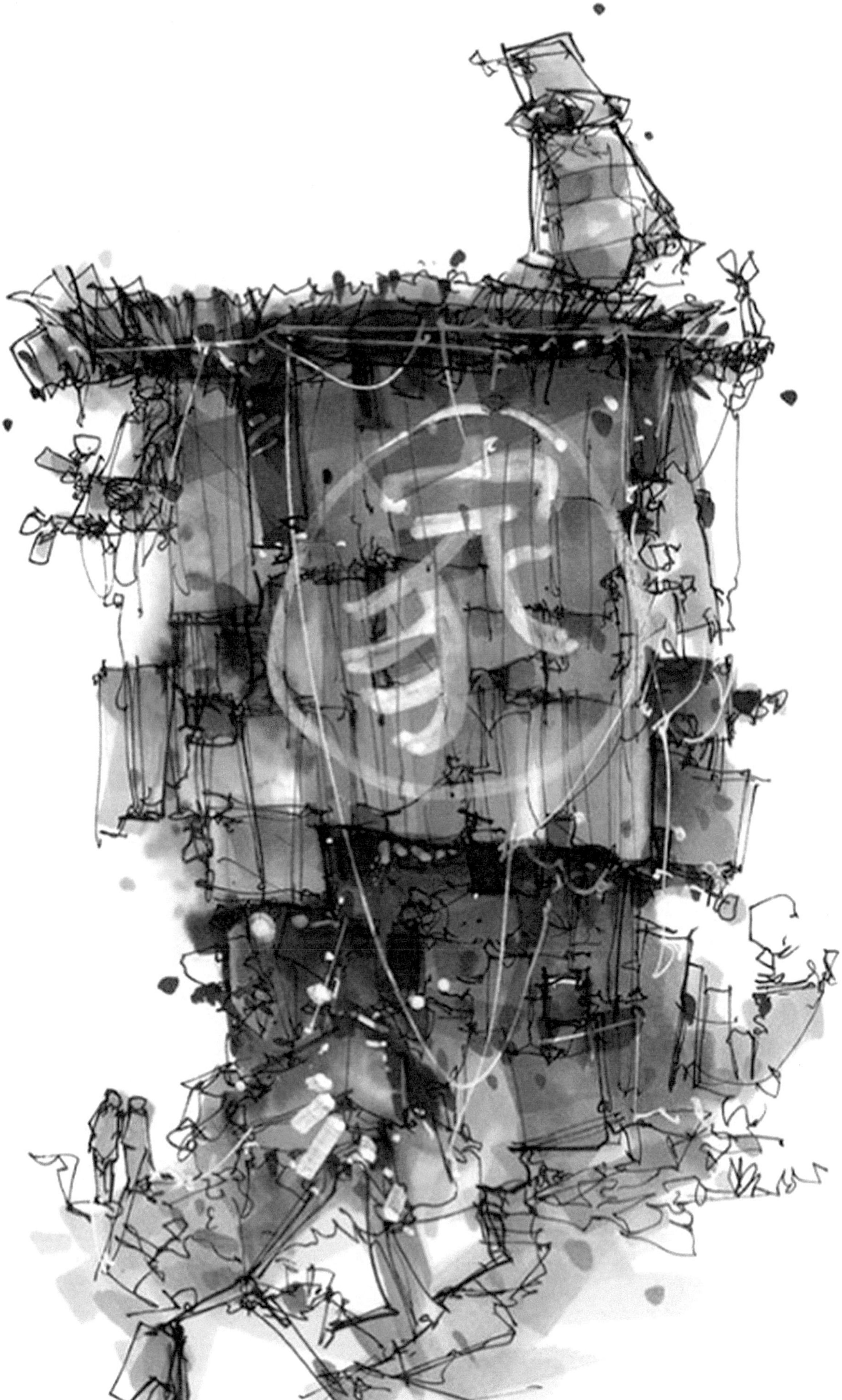

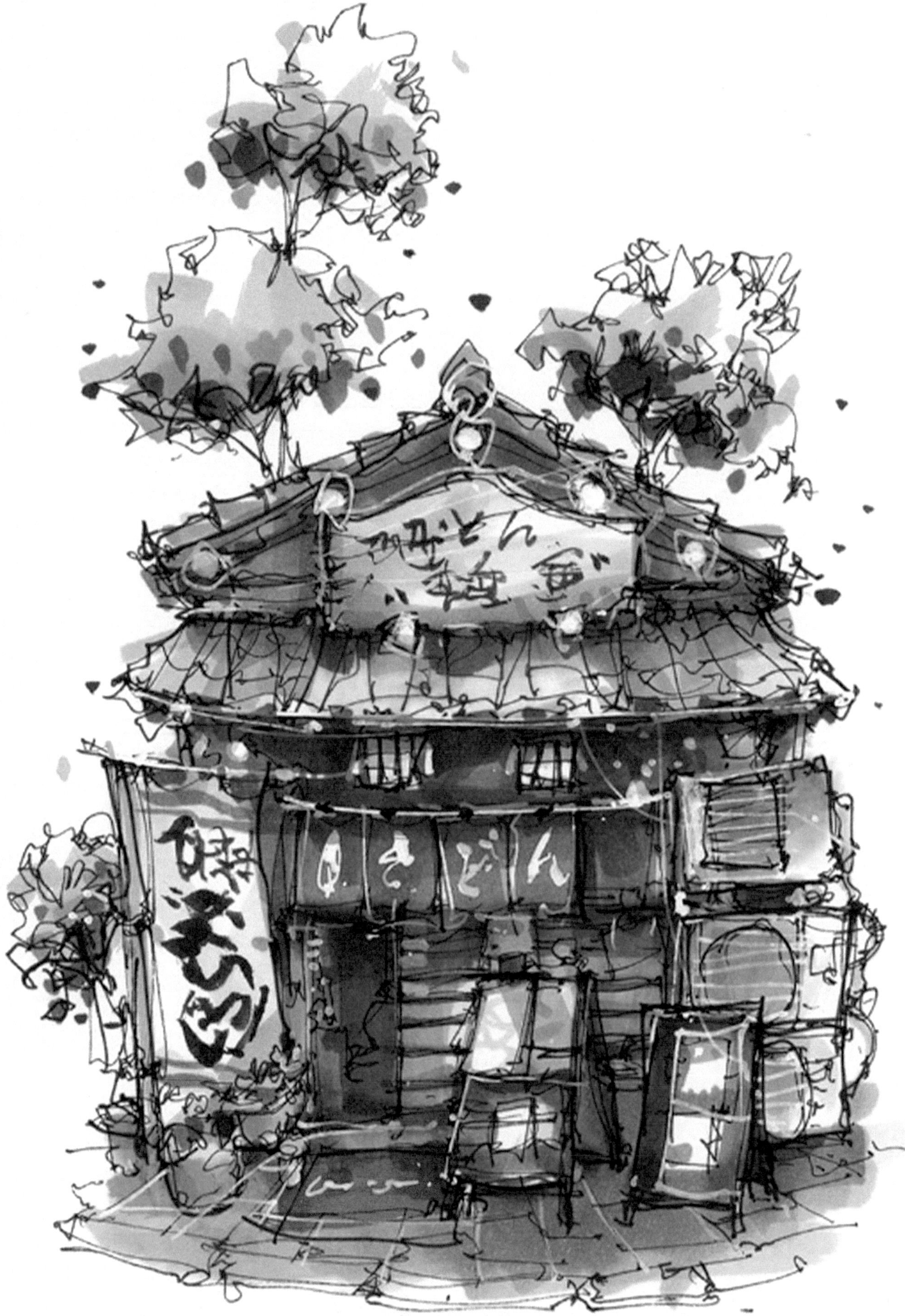

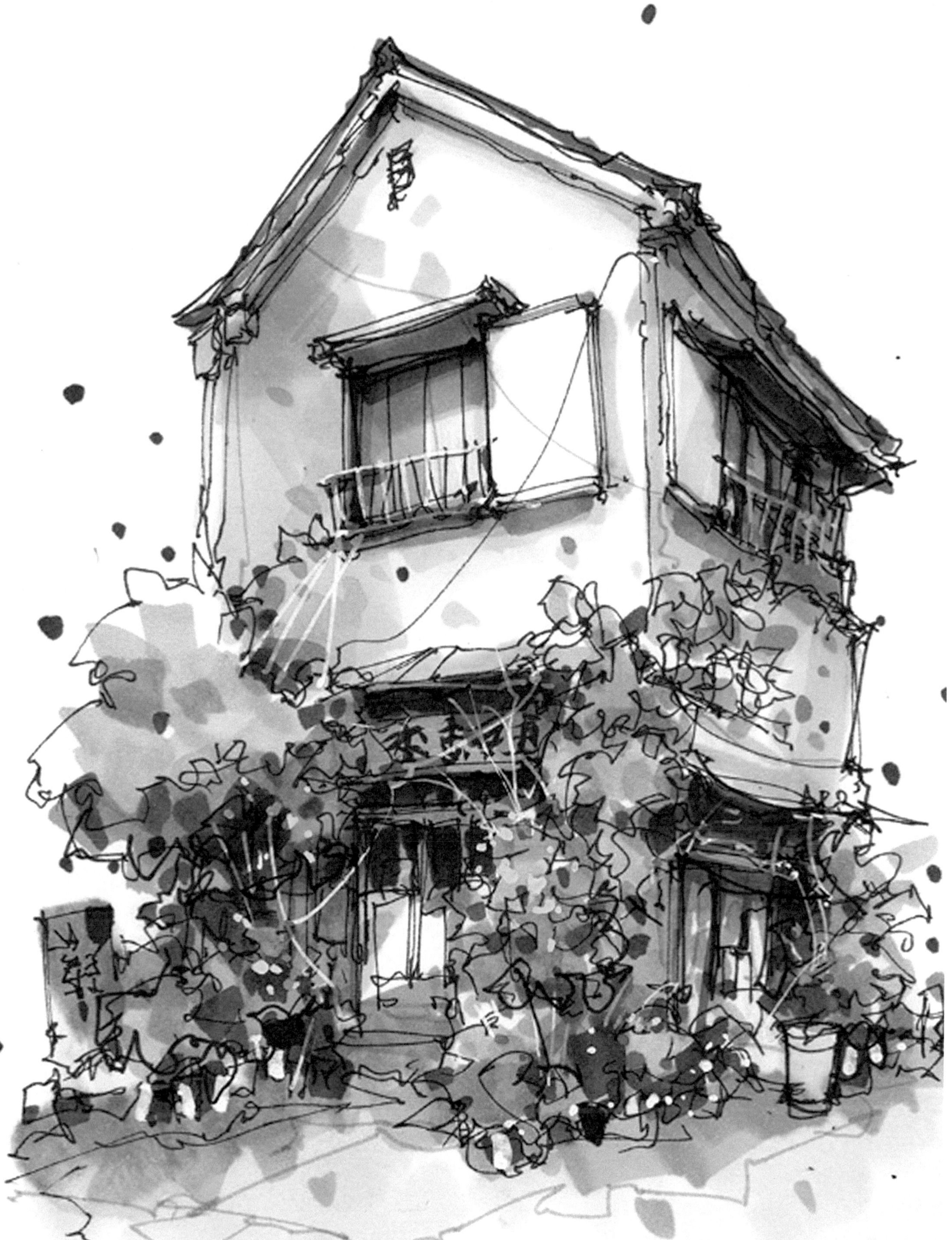

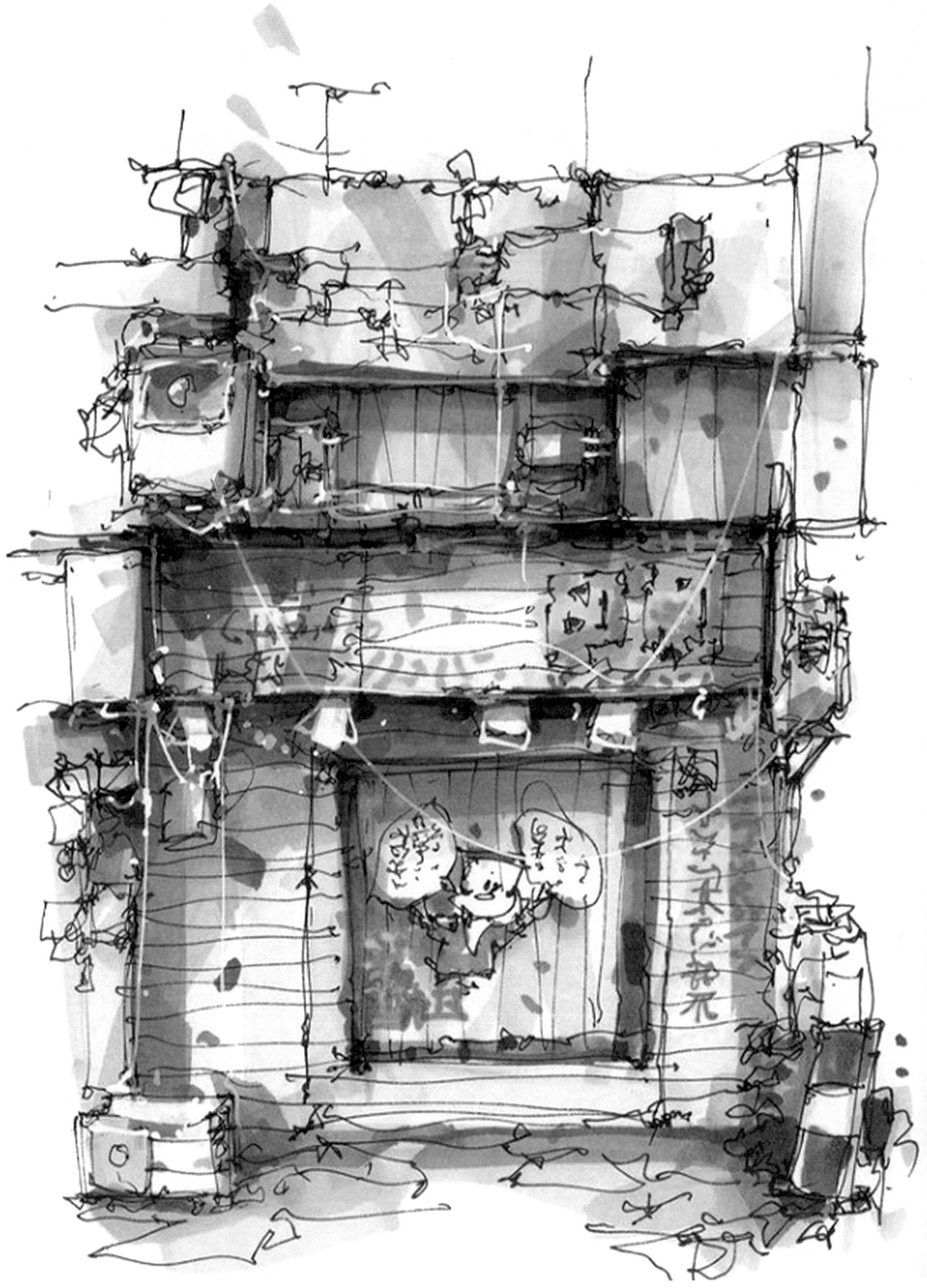

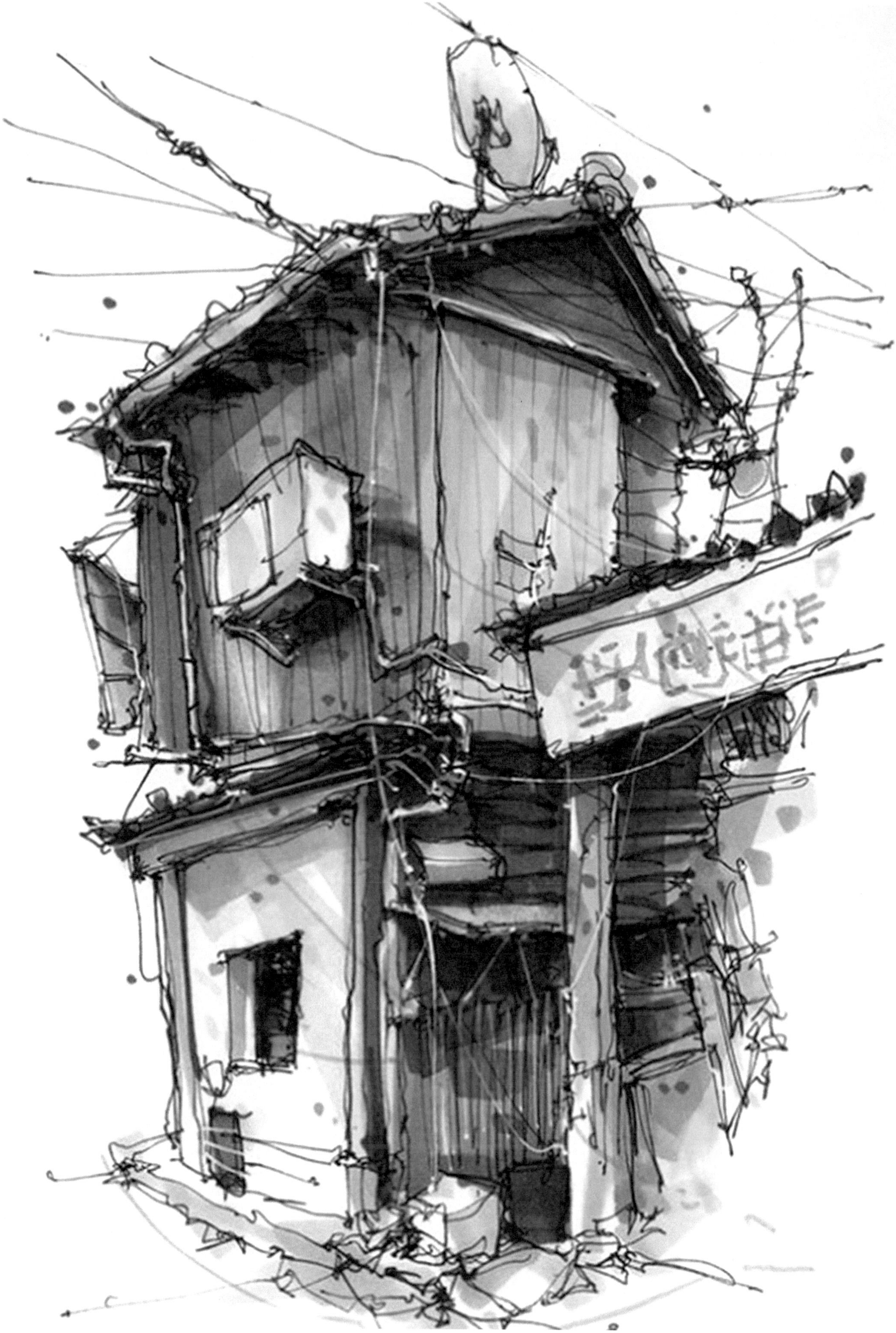

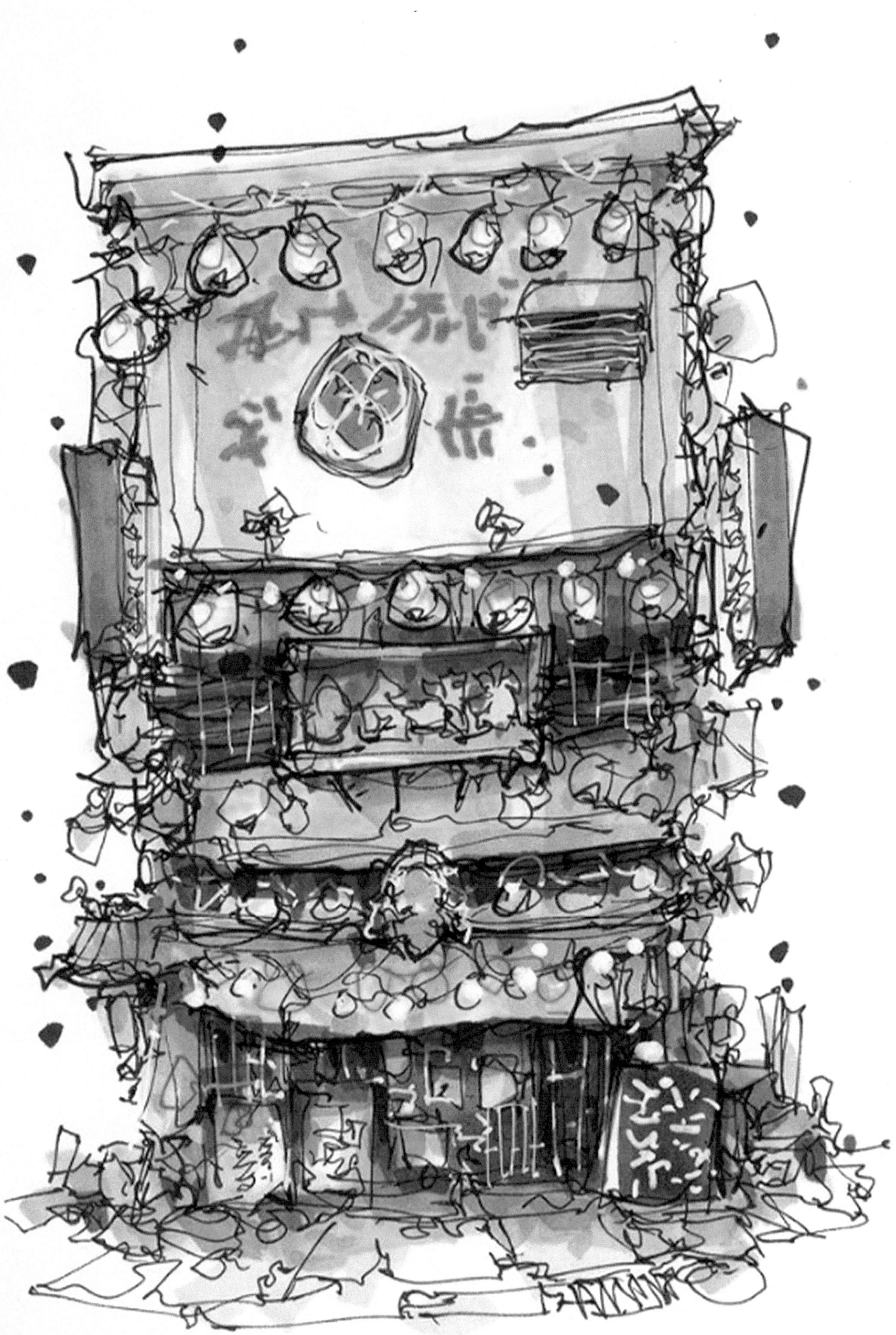

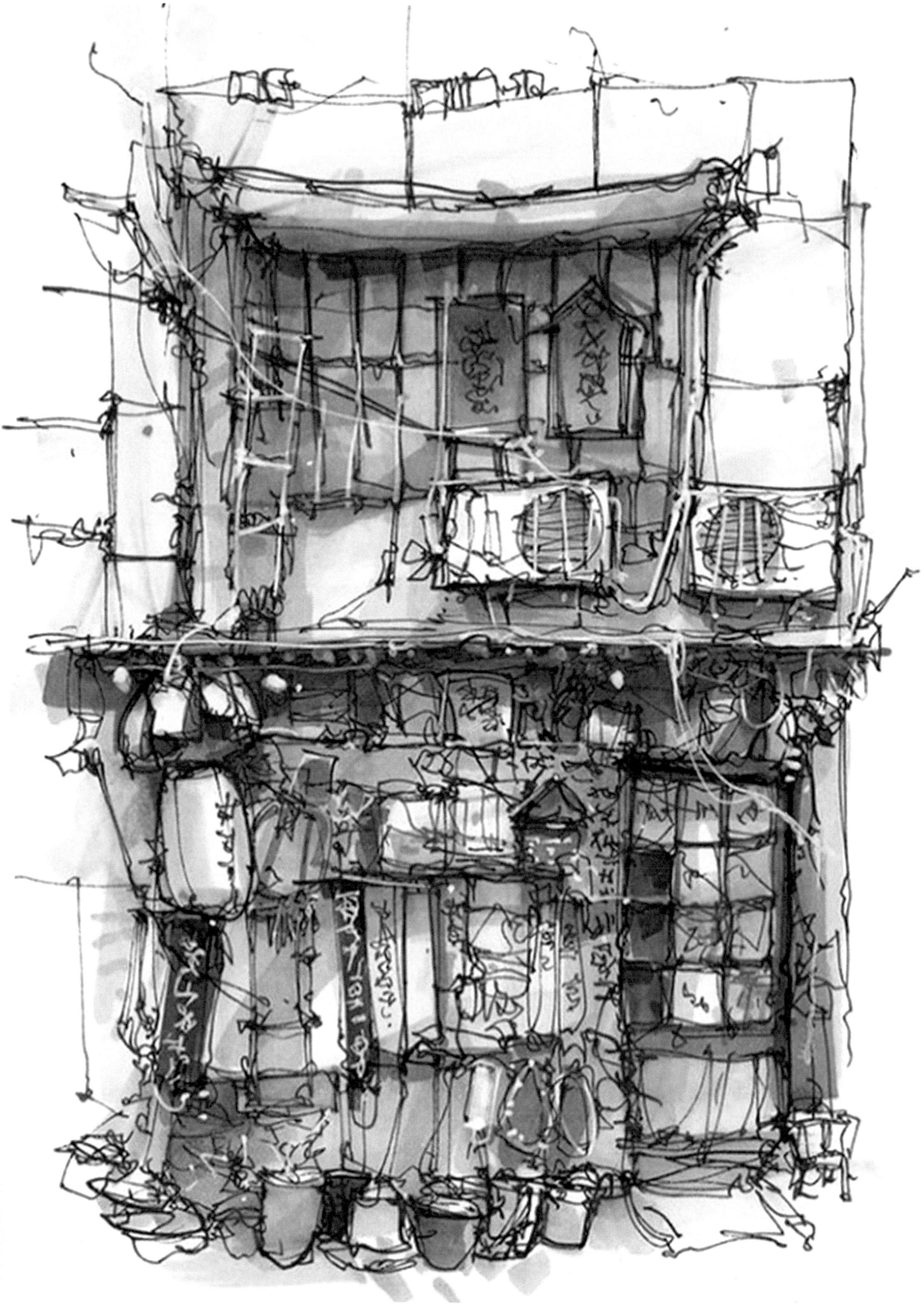

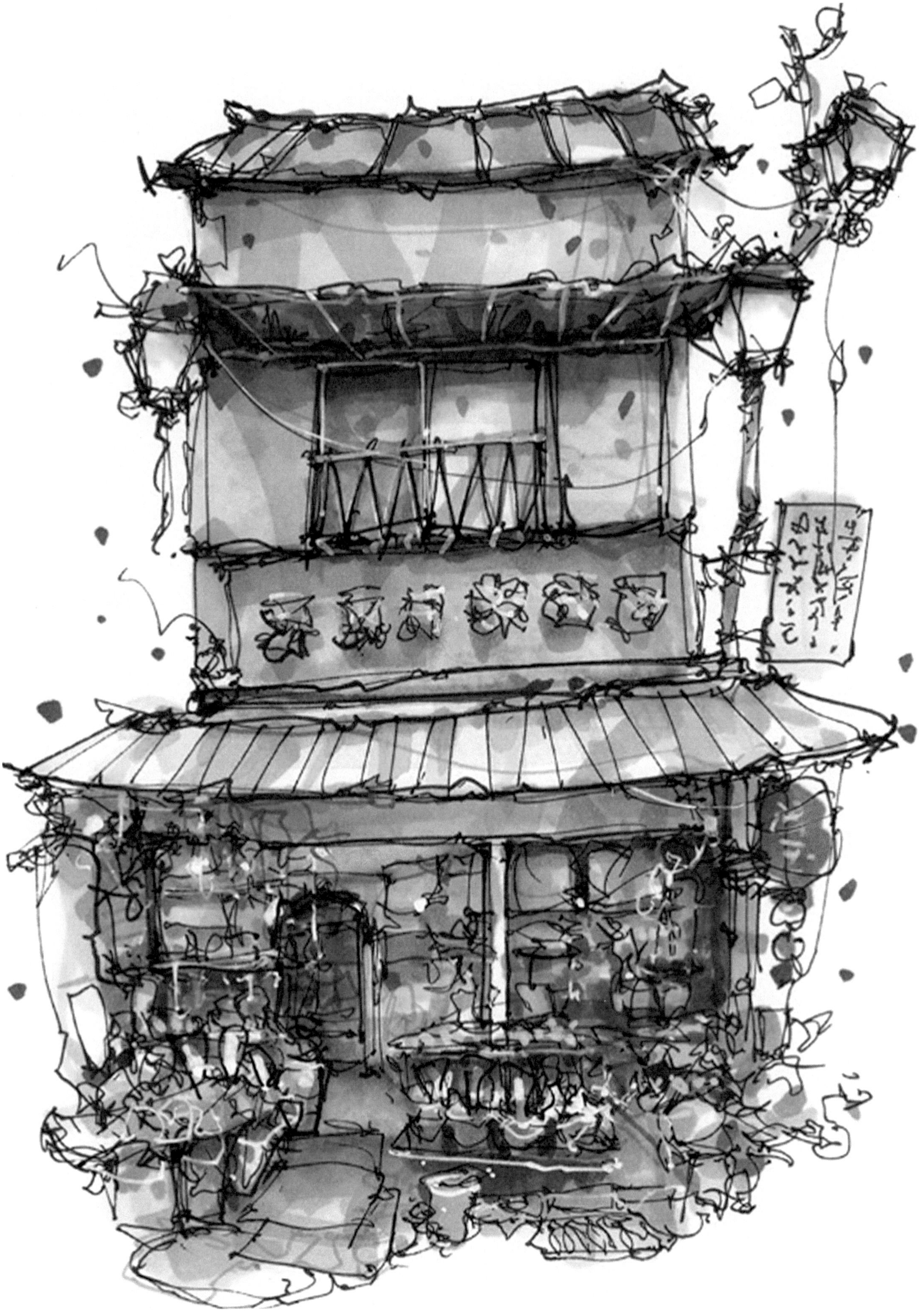

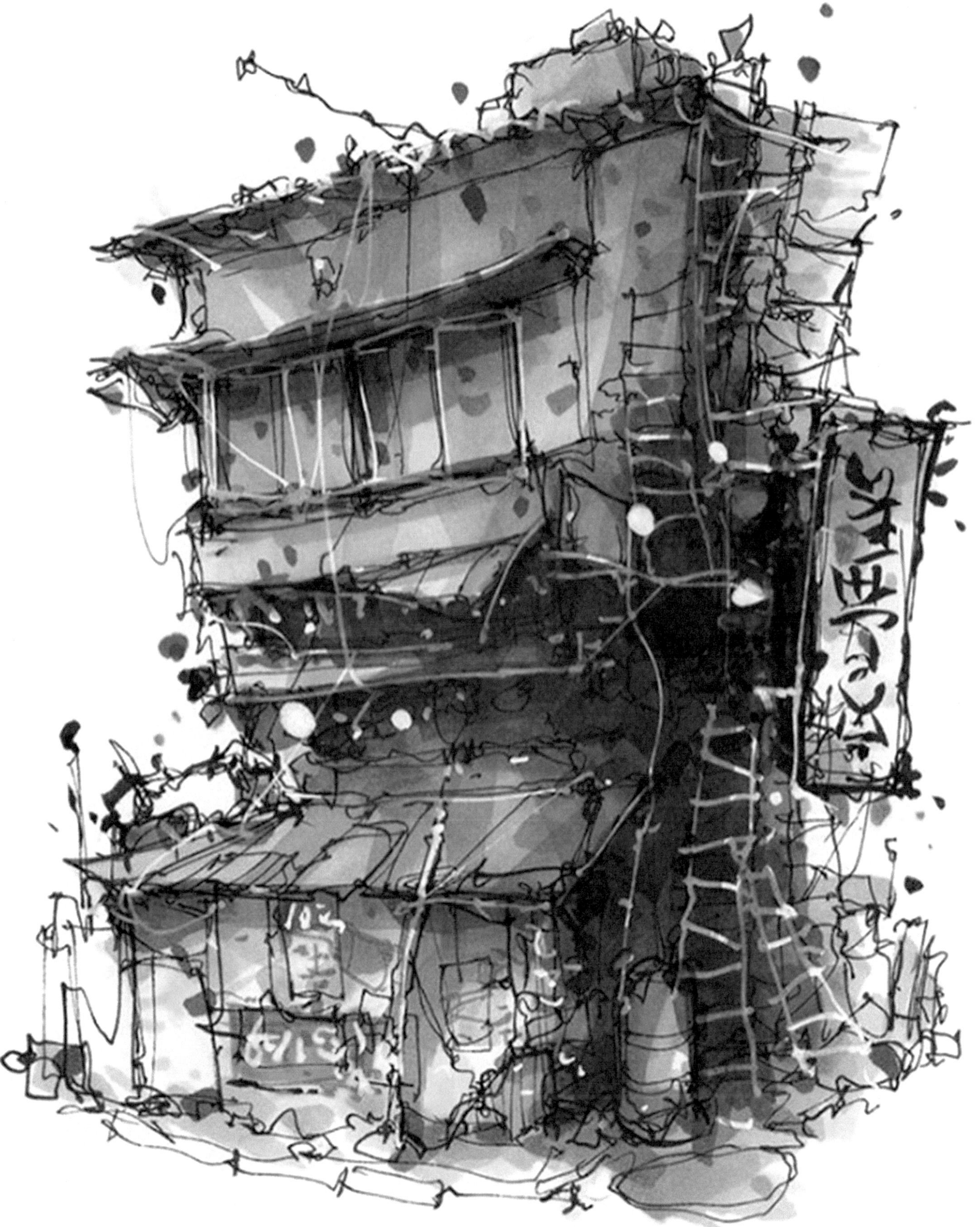

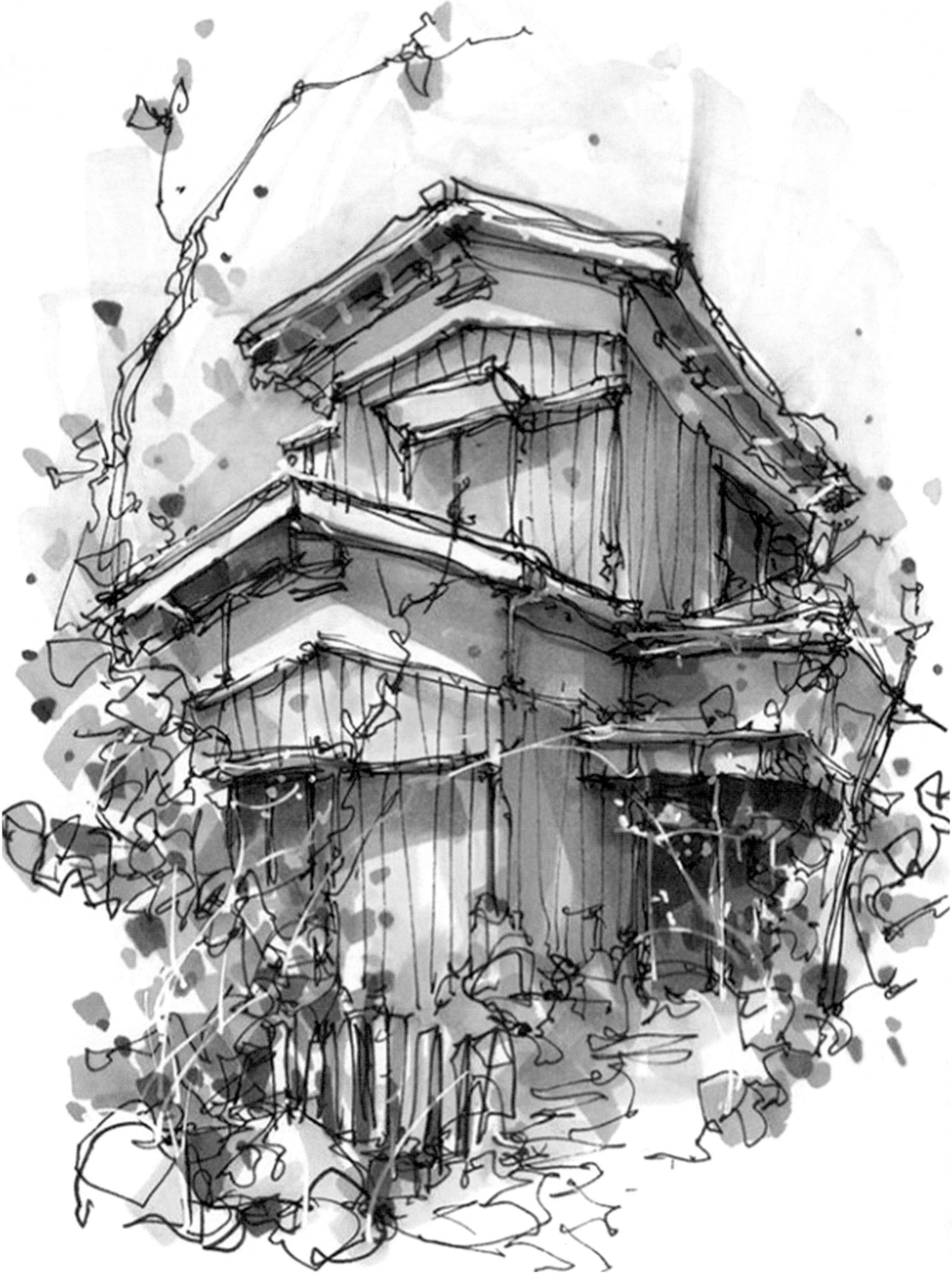

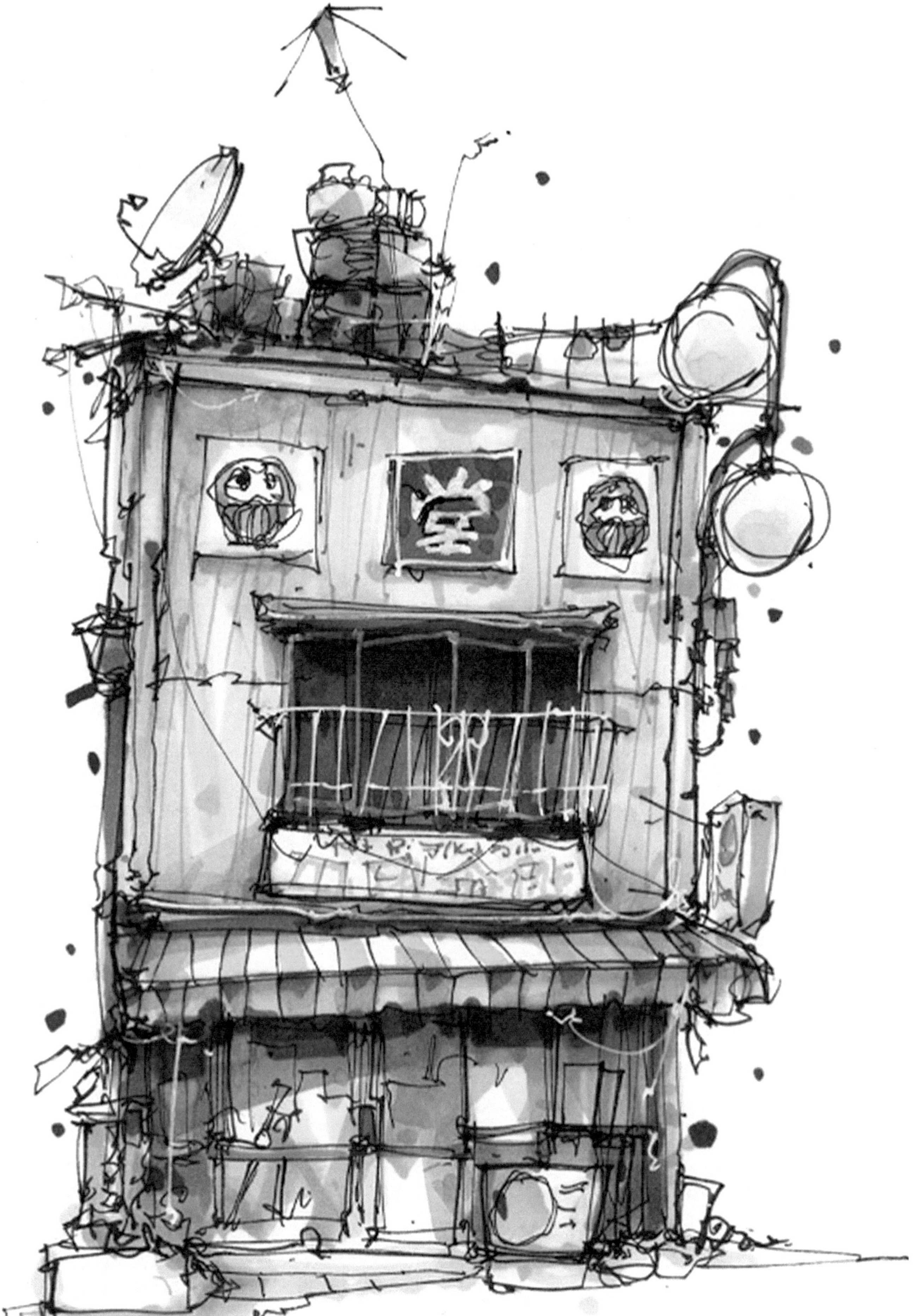

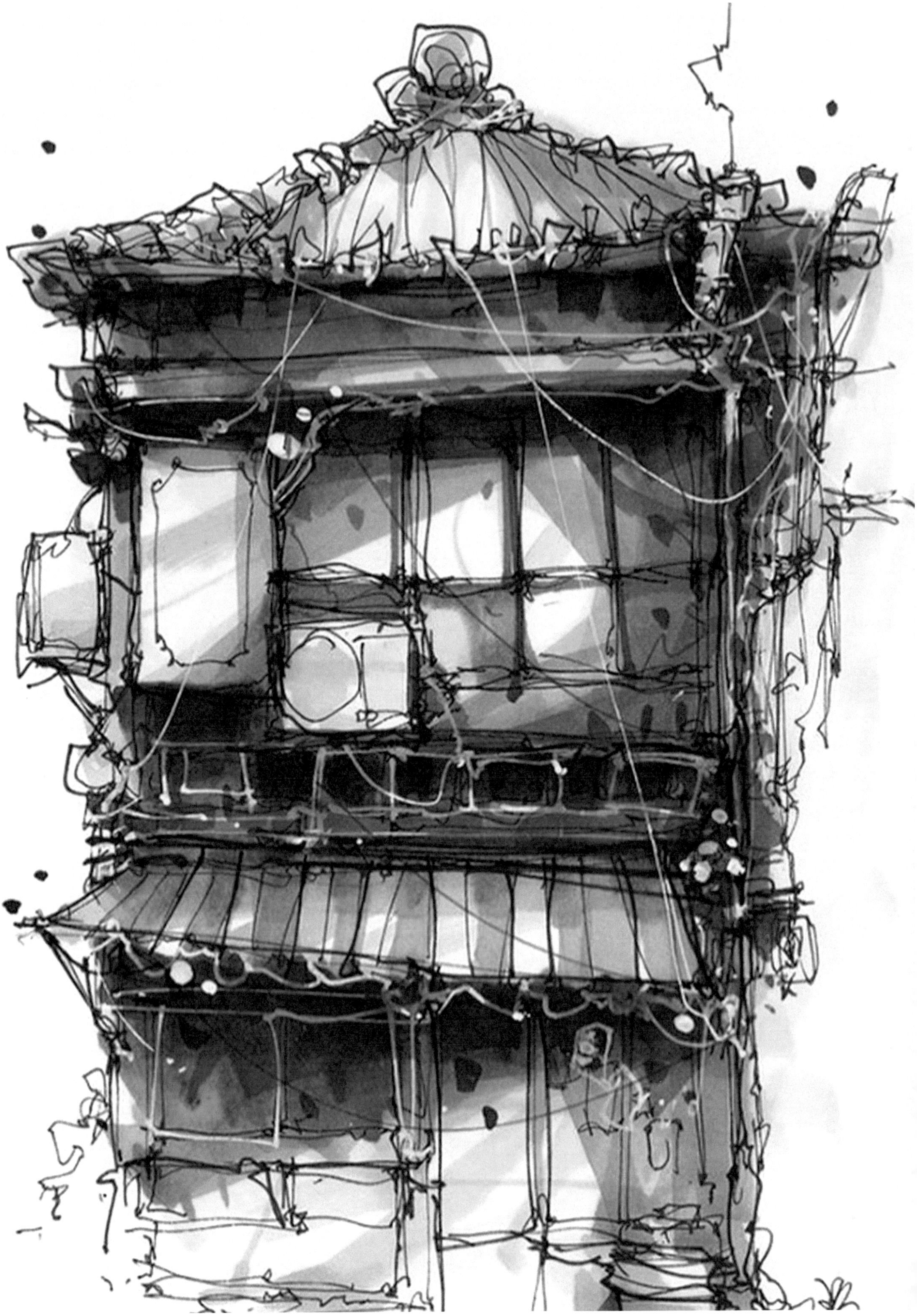

Made in the USA
Thornton, CO
11/06/24 20:00:58

9a0f94f2-0c9c-4877-b1c4-9b6f607b8daaR02